Theoretical Background of Asian Regionalization and the Changing of the World System

―from Environmental, Financial and Economical Facets―

Hideaki KAWATO

Contents

Chapter 1　Introduction ··8
　　　　　(1) The main theme of this thesis
　　　　　(2) The Analytical method
　　　　　(3) The antecedent research and writings

Chapter 2　The theoretical history of International Political Economy····················11
　Section 1　From Mercantilism to Economic Liberalism·········11
　　　　　(1) Mercantilism
　　　　　(2) The Mercantilist Period of History
　　　　　(3) Distribution of Wealth and Economic Activities
　　　　　(4) Roots of the Liberal Perspective
　Section 2　Keynesian and Hegemonic Stability·········17
　　　　　(1) Keynes
　　　　　(2) Hegemonic stability
　Section 3　The Politics of International Regimes·········20
　Section 4　Marxism, Dependency and World System Theory·········23
　　　　　(1) Marx and History
　　　　　(2) Modern World System Theory
　　　　　(3) Dependency Theory

Chapter 3　The rise of Globalization ··29
　Section 1　The changing of world economic order·········29
　Section 2　The benefits and critics of Globalization·········34
　　　　　(1) Benefits
　　　　　(2) The critics
　Section 3　The international trade regime·········39
　　　　　(1) Postwar Trade Regime
　　　　　(2) The Uruguay Round and World Trade Organization

Chapter 4　The rise of Asian regionalism ···45
　Section 1　The experience of Asian financial crisis·········45
　Section 2　The promotion of regional trade·········48
　　　　　(1) Bilateral trade agreement
　　　　　(2) Bilateral trade agreements as positional goods

Section 3　Chinese economic development………51
　　　　　(1) China and other Asian countries
　　　　　(2) The Challenges Ahead
　　　　　(3) Governance for Social and Economic Development
　　　　　(4) Environmental Sustainability and Energy Conservation

Chapter 5　The three theoretical facets of Asian regionalism ……………………56
　Section 1　Global environmental crisis………56
　　　　　(1) Growing population
　　　　　(2) Tragedy of Freedom in a Commons
　　　　　(3) Pollution
　　　　　(4) How to Legislate Temperance
　　　　　(5) Freedom to Breed Is Intolerable
　　　　　(6) Conscience Is Self-Eliminating
　　　　　(7) Pathogenic Effects of Conscience
　　　　　(8) Mutual Coercion, Mutually Agreed Upon
　　　　　(9) Recognition of Necessity
　Section 2　South-To-North cooperation in Asia………67
　　　　　(1) The Types of Economic Cooperation
　　　　　(2) Cooperation between ASEAN and China
　Section 3　Monetary policy of China and other Asian countries………69
　　　　　(1) Costs and Benefits of the Currency Peg
　　　　　(2) What Kind of New Regime?
　　　　　(3) Anchoring Monetary Policy
　　　　　(4) Implications for Other Asian Countries

Chapter 6　The regional cooperation in Europe ……………………………………96
　Section 1　The reason to stick together for the future………96
　Section 2　The practical system of European Monetary System………98
　　　　　(1) The European Monetary System
　　　　　(2) The EMS as a Coordinating Device
　　　　　(3) Government Accountability in the EMS: An Empirical Examination
　Section 3　The impact of EURO………102
　　　　　(1) European financial markets and the euro
　　　　　(2) International role of the euro

Chapter 7　Globalization and Governance ……………………………………………105
　Section 1　The movement of Hegemony………105

    (1) The U.S. power

    (2) After the September 11

  Section 2 International organizations and its role·········110

  Section 3 Triangle balance of power·········113

    (1) The Functions of Regionalism

    (2) 21st Century Global Geopolitical Change

Chapter 8 The future of Asian Regional cooperation ·····································119

  Section1 Current situation·········119

    (1) China-ASEAN FTA

    (2) Japan on FTA with ASEAN

    (3) Major Southeast Asian Powers

    (4) India as a New Element in East Asian regionalization

    (5) Obstacles to the APT Process

  Section 2 Chinese financial instability.·········124

    (1) Bad Debt

    (2) Interest rate rise

  Section 3 Security problem·········128

    (1) Stabilization under Uni-polar Structure Led by U.S.

    (2) Destabilization by Multi-polar Structure －Probable Change by around 2030－

    (3) Moves of Main Powers by 2030

    (4) Changing Threat Aspect to Japan

  Section 4 Monetary system·········135

    (1) The Problem of an Asian Monetary Union

    (2) Prospects of the APT Process

Chapter9 Conclusion ···139

Bibliography ··142

Abbreviations and Acronyms

ACFTA	ASEAN China Free Trade Agreement
ADB	Asian Development Bank
AEM	ASEAN Economic Ministers Meeting
AKFTA	ASEAN Korea Free Trade Agreement
APEC	Asia-Pacific Economic Cooperation
APT	Asia-Pacific Telecommunity
ASEAN	Association of South-East Asian Nations
BIS	Bank for International Settlements
CIA	Central Intelligence Agency
CMI	Chiang Mai Initiative
COMECON	Council for Mutual Economic Assistance
EAS	East Asia Summit
ECSC	European Coal and Steel Community
EEC	European Economic Community
EMS	European Monetary System
ERM	European Exchange Rate Mechanism
EU	European Union
EURATOM	European Atomic Energy Community
FDI	Foreign Direct Investment
FTA	Free Trade Agreement
GATT	General Agreement on Tariffs and Trade
GDP	Gross Domestic Product
IFS	International Financial Statistics
IMF	International Monetary Fund
IPE	International Political Economy
ITO	International Trade Organization
LDCs	Less Developed Countries
MDGs	Millennium Development Goals
MERCOSUR	Mercado Comun del Sur
MNCs	Multi-National Corporations
MWS	Modern World System
NAFTA	North American Free Trade Agreement
NATO	North Atlantic Treaty Organization

NGO	Non-governmental Organization
NICs	Newly Industrializing Countries
NIEO	New International Economic Order
NIEs	Newly Industrializing Economies
NMD	National Missile Defense
NPLs	Non-performing loans
ODA	Official Development Assistance
OPEC	Organization of the Petroleum Exporting Countries
PBOC	People's Bank of China
QDR	Quadrennial Defense Review
RMB	Renminbi
UN	United Nations
UNCTAD	United Nations Conference on Trade and Development
USSR	Union of Soviet Socialist Republics
WB	World Bank
WMD	Weapons of Mass Destruction
WTO	World Trade Organization

Chapter 1　Introduction

(1) The main theme of this thesis

Since the end of the Cold War, globalization has been the most outstanding characteristic of international economic affairs and, to a considerable extent, of political affairs as well. After the rise of globalization, the world has experienced many events. As the result of the M&A which were done by a great number of companies with the intensification of competition, the reorganization of various industries has taken place. And also it was discovered that costs can be held down in Asia. Especially, economic development in China took large steps toward it becoming an advanced nation. A globalized world also promoted stronger regional relationship in the world. The EU made a common currency and urged a single market. It is a notable and advanced regional union with 10 new members. On the other hand, the United States, the hegemonic country, did not have the assent of world public opinion regarding the Iraq war. Consequently, the economic development of other regions made their position lower. However, the existence of the United States remains important as the world's largest economic power holder. Thus, at the regional cooperation, they have the initiative on NATO or APEC. In other words, it is now difficult for United States to exercise their hegemony alone and we can say that they are seeking their role in the regionalization. This stream of regionalization can be divided into 3 parts: Europe, Asia and North and South America. Especially, the Asian regionalization is considerable because of Asian's economic influence on the world. This research concentrates on the Asian regionalization. As for the causes of regionalization, I will examine the historical background of globalization and the theoretical background of regionalization. As a result of my research, I predict that regional cooperation will become the central component of the future's new world system. In addition, I discuss the monetary union that Asian region will develop via comparison with the example of the EURO.

(2) The Analytical method

Presently in Asia, Asian countries try to build up closer cooperation to prevent another financial crisis and to promote stable economic development. The development of such regional cooperation connects with the building of new international relations in the 21st century. This will also be an important element in the international relations and the international political economy theory.

In my research, I examine both the background and the future of the construction of the system of finance and economic cooperation in Asia. Therefore, this thesis utilizes 3 corner theories to support the inevitability of the world to advance towards the regional bloc.

Firstly, it verifies a regional bloc with the biological approach from the Lifeboat Theory by Garrett Hardin. He predicted that human beings will chose the regional union to survive from the global ecological disaster which is currently a serious problem in the world. Therefore, it should address the current ecological problem which can be solved with cooperation among the member states in the region.

Secondly, then it suggests the advanced theory from World System Theory by Immanuel Wallerstein. This theory is based on the theory called Dependency Theory which says the world became divided into core and peripheral nations, and since then the core nations have exploited the peripheral nations. He has added the concept of semi-peripheral nations.

Finally, it verifies the monetary union will make the ideal structure for the international currency system in the future the theory by Barry Eichengreen that the floating exchange system or monetary union will have to be chosen as the currency system by most of all countries in the future.

On these three theories, this thesis analyzes former processes and the present situation in Asia, and makes clear the stake among the major countries in Asia which are charged with an important role in its development as a world power. Then it argues about the future development and evaluation of the system which is achieved in the present step. Also, the relationship between Japan and China will be one of the important elements for creating Asian regional cooperation, so it estimates the view of this cooperative relationship between countries. Moreover, because the relationship has a great influence on the Asian economy regarding the problem of the Chinese bubble economy, and currency problem, I advance about the policy what the Asian countries, particularly Japan, should do comprehensively. Next, it reviews about the ideal concepts of the policy to the outside of the Asian region. Especially, to analyze the convergence and the development in Asia it is practical to study the case s in the EU as one of the advanced regional block, Finally, it verifies whether or not the applications are possible.

(3) **The antecedent research and writings**

Many researches about the transfiguration of the world system and globalization・regionalization have been carried out, such as D.S. Wright, R. Gilpin, S Gill, R. Higgott and so on. Many important pieces of research about regionalization and globalization have been done at the Centre for the Study of Globalisation and Regionalisation in University of Warwick. However, regionalization is generally considered as an opposed globalization and studies have been made mainly upon the conflict between them in the context of a cost and benefit analysis. Few studies have taken on the regionalization as a phenomenon coincidentally developed with the globalization. It is hardly possible to explain why the formation of regional economic communities has been accelerated along with the development of globalization. Issues also remain in the analytical framework of these preceding studies. Many studies have been made either within a purely political analysis associated with issues of hegemony as for the formation of an economic block or a purely mechanical economic analysis on the matter. The consequence is a tendency to leave unexplored the common ground where the two overlap and interrelate, especially the matters relevant to the structural change in the world system.

Bearing these in mind, this essay will examine the recent wave of regionalization and the structural transformation of the world system in a politico-economic analysis with the axes of examination on the movement of regionalization in Asia.

My antecedent researches and writings relating to the matter are included in this essay as integral parts. My master's thesis was on "The economic and political significance of European Monetary Union - fixing the influence on the reorganizing world monetary system —" Furthermore, my master course taken at the University of Warwick, gave me enough bases on international political economy which is required for the further development of the studies.

Based on this study, I have developed researches and examinations on the formation of regional economic communities and the transfiguration of the world system in the doctorial course work.

Chapter 2 The theoretical history of International Political Economy

Section1 From Mercantilism to Economic Liberalism

(1) **Mercantilism**

In the past, the term mercantilism accounted for the desire of states to generate trade surpluses to increase their wealth. To the extent that wealth enhanced a state's military power by producing or purchasing weapons, it enhanced national security as well. Mercantilism is also the name given to a historical period when the major European powers colonized much of the "New World". As it did earlier, neo-mercantilism today accounts for compulsion of states to use the economy to generate wealth but also to adopt a variety of protectionist trade, investment, and other policies to sustain that wealth and to condition the behavior of other states.

Neo-mercantilism remains a potent force, often manifested in protectionist policies some states adopt to counter the benign neo-mercantilist policies of other nations. Given the compulsion of nation-states to think or act on the basis of the national interest, policymakers will continue to be guided by mercantilist tendencies.

Typically, mercantilism is defined somewhat narrowly in terms of states efforts to promote exports and limit imports, thereby gene, rating trade surpluses to create wealth and power.

Mercantilism can refer to the sixteenth through mid-nineteenth century practice of states pursuing supremacy over one another by accumulating gold and silver bullion, colonizing developing regions of the world, and trying to generates trade surpluses. In the emerging competing nation-states system of Western and Central Europe, governments added to their military arsenals a variety of economic instruments and policies to protect themselves and/or groups within their jurisdiction. Since then, a variety of terms have become synonymous with the idea of mercantilism: namely, economic nationalism, realism, neo-mercantilism, and power to protect their industries and an assortment of other national interests.

(2) **The Mercantilist Period of History**

The period from the sixteenth through the eighteenth centuries is designated as the period of mercantilism, when the major European states explored, conquered, and colonized large tracts of the New World in search of gold, silver, and other precious metals. The mercantilist period corresponds to the deepening entrenchment of the nation-state as the major sovereign political actor on the European continent. A nation is a collection of people who, on the basis of ethnic background, language, and history, define themselves as members of an extended political community. The state is a legal entity, theoretically free of external interference, that monopolizes the means of physical force in society and that exercises sovereignty (final political authority) over the population of a well-defined territory.[1]

The modern nation-state merges social-psychological and political phenomena into a single actor above which there is no higher sovereign in the international state system. Nation-states as we think of them today first appeared in Europe in the fifteenth century. Soon after Venice and other Italian city-states, together with Portugal, Spain, the Netherlands, France, England, and a number of weaker powers, formed a system of states and fought long wars with one another. To help pay for their wars, these states tried to accumulate trade surpluses by promoting exports and limiting imports. Currency earned from trade helped them purchase gold and silver bullion, much of it imported from the New World, which was added to the monarch's treasury. Because commerce and exploration were so important, the Dutch, Spanish, and British all competed with one another to build ships and rule the seas. Sea-power became as important, if not more so, than land-based military power. Commerce-generated wealth enhanced the nation's power, which the major powers believed ultimately made them more secure in relation to one another. Economic gains by one state were perceived by competing states as losses, conferring on mercantilism a zero-sum disposition to account for heavy state competition for resources that generated wealth and power.

The mercantilist period coincides with what Marxists and others structuralists refer to as classical imperialism, when stronger nations ventured overseas in search of gold and other precious metals. Conquered territories became colonies and provided their mother countries with raw materials and labor. As was the case of the American colonies that had to purchase and pay a tax on British tea, colonies were often forced to purchase some of the mother country's value-added products. And many were forbidden to produce semi-manufactured or manufactured goods of their own that competed with the products of the mother country. At home, many states adopted policies to complement their colonial practices. States emphasized exported goods because they were cheaper to ship and often earned high prices in foreign markets. Many absolute rulers of the period limited spending for imported goods and used treasury founds to encourage the production of goods for export. For example, King Louis XVI's minister, Jean-Baptiste Colbert (1619-1683), imported ship builders from Holland to build ships, built seaports, financed road construction, and provided tax exemptions and subsidies to exporters of some of France's most expensive items such as silk, tapestries, and glassware.

For over three centuries, mercantilism helped concentrate wealth and power into the hands of a few European nations. For better or for worse, increasing trade between European powers and their colonies helped entrench economic interdependence (interconnectedness) among them. The stronger European powers gradually settled down into a relatively stable military balance of power among themselves.

In the late eighteenth century, mercantilism receded in influence corresponding to, among other things, the increasing popularity of economic liberal ideas associated with Adam Smith and David Ricardo. Smith and Ricardo preached to English policymakers, academics, and businessmen the benefits of free trade and a laissez-faire role for the state in the economy. Liberalism's popularity paralleled at least three significant developments in Europe. First, England ascended to the position of hegemon—dominant economic and military power—in the European state system. British maritime power shifted from one of support of one continental power to that of helping maintain a balance of power among the European nations. Second, the industrial revolution took place first in England, which gave it an advantage over its continental competitors in producing gods at cheaper prices. Third and finally, at this juncture of history, the absolute power of the monarch was weakened. A number of European monarchs were gradually compelled to share power with relatively democratic bodies such as a parliament. Spurred on by the French Revolution and Napoleonic wars, the eighteenth through twentieth centuries experienced a change: the overriding economic and political goals of states gradually shifted from increasing the power of the monarchy and merchant class to improving the well-being of an entire nation's population. More often, governments contracted with the people to provide for their security and welfare in exchange for their financial support of state institutions and loyalty to the fatherland. Nationalistic feelings spread throughout the continent and became another driving force behind the state's desire to influence developments in the economy.

(3) Distribution of Wealth and Economic Activities

The significance of relative gains for economic behavior and in the calculations of nation-states was recognized at least as early as the economic writings of the eighteenth-century political philosopher David Hume (1711-1776). Hume's mercantilist contemporaries argued that a nation should seek a trade and payments surplus, basing their arguments on the assumption that it was only relative gains that really mattered. In today's language of game theory, international commerce during the mercantilist era was considered to be a zero-sum game in which the gain to one party necessarily meant a loss to another. Hume himself demonstrated the folly and self-defeating nature of this mercantilist argument by introducing the "price-specie flow mechanism" into economic thought.[2] Subsequently, formulation by David Ricardo (1772-1823) of the law or principle of comparative advantage revealed that every nation could gain in absolute terms from free trade and from an international division of labor based on territorial specialization. Subsequent modifications of Ricardo's theory suggested that states were also interested in the relative gains from trade. Ricardo's demonstration that international economic exchange was not a zero-sum game but rather a positive-sum game from which everyone could gain led Paul Samuelson to call the law of comparative advantage "the most beautiful idea" in economic science. However, both absolute gains and the distribution of those gains are important in international economic affairs.

A number of political economists have addressed the issue of absolute versus relative gains in international affairs, and the ensuing debate has largely centered on Joseph Grieco's argument that states are more concerned about relative than absolute gains and that this creates difficulties in attaining international cooperation.[3]

Whereas many scholars stress the importance of relative gains, liberals emphasize the importance of absolute gains. Absolute gains, they argue, are more important than Grieco's analysis suggests, and therefore international cooperation should be easier to attain than he postulates. While Grieco's emphasis on the importance of relative gains is basically important, and states do, in general, prize relative gains, sometimes even at the expense of absolute gains, this argument cannot be elevated into a general law of state behavior.

The importance of absolute versus relative gains in state calculations is actually highly dependent upon the circumstances in which a specific trade-off occurs. While it may be true that states can never be totally unconcerned about the distributive consequences of economic activities for their relative wealth and power, they frequently ignore this concern in their dealings with others for largely security reasons. During the height of Cold War, for example, the United States fostered the economic unification of Western Europe for political reasons despite the cost to its own economic interest. Kenneth Waltz has noted that the conscious decision of the United States in the late 1940s to build the power of its European allies at a sacrifice to itself was historically on unprecedented action.

States are particularly interested in the distribution of those gains affecting domestic welfare, national wealth, and military power. When a state weighs absolute versus relative gains, military power is by far the most important consideration; states are extraordinarily reluctant, for example, to trade military security for economic gains. Modern nation-states (like eighteenth-century mercantilists) are extremely concerned about the consequences of international economic activities for the distribution of economic gains. Over time, the unequal distribution of these gains will inevitably change the international balance of economic and military power, and will thus affect national security. For this reason, states have always been very sensitive to the effects of the international economy on relative rates of economic growth. At the beginning of the twenty-first century, concern is focused on the distribution of industrial power, especially in those high-tech industries vitally important to the relative power position of individual states. The territorial distribution of industry and of technological capabilities is a matter of great concern for every state and a major issue in the international political economy.

(4) Roots of the Liberal Perspective

Liberalism is "a simple, dramatic philosophy. Its central idea is liberty under the law."[4] The liberal point of view reveals clearly some parts of political economy that mercantilists miss, but necessarily loses other valuable insights in the shadows.

The liberal perspective focuses on the side of human nature that is peaceful and cooperative, competitive in a constructive way, and guided by reason, not emotion. To the extent that individuals and states behave in this way, the liberal perspective holds. Although liberals believe that people are fundamentally self-interested, they do not see this as a disadvantage because they think that broad areas of society are set up in such a way so that competitors can all gain, through peaceful and cooperative actions. This contrasts with the mercantilist view, which dwells on the side of human nature that is more aggressive, combative, and suspicious.

While the cooperative side of human nature is highlighted by the liberal perspective, it tends to focus on the abusive aspects of the state. Indeed, it might not be too strong to consider liberalism as an anti-state school of thought. Early liberals condemned the abuses of state authority and promoted reforms, such as democratic systems of government, that weakened central power while promoting individual liberty. The dual nature of liberal thought—embracing individual liberty and being wary of state abuses—is fundamental to liberalism and can be seen clearly in the earlier quotations from Smith and Havel.

It is easy to imagine why one might fear state abuses; one need only read the U.S. Declaration of Independence to gain an appreciation of this side of liberalism. But it may be more difficult to appreciate the liberal tendency to view individual actions as cooperative and constructive, not competitive and destructive. In the jargon of political economy, liberals think that society is a positive-sum game. In a positive-sum game, everyone can potentially get more out of a bargain that they put in. Love is one example of a positive-sum game, and market exchange of goods or services that are mutually advantageous is another. Mercantilists tend to view life as a zero-sum game, where gains by one person or group necessarily come at the expense of others.

Liberals view the fundamental tension between state and market as a conflict between coercion and freedom, authority and individual rights, autocratic dogma and rational logic. Appalled by the abuses of church and states authority dating from feudal days, the early liberals saw a kind of salvation in individual freedom, voluntary association, and rational thought. The market, in their view, was an admirable distillation of the values and characteristics that they advanced.

The liberal view, then, comes down heavily on the side of the market when choosing sides between states and market, a fundamental tension that characterized by the phrase lasses-faire. Free individuals are best equipped to make social choices. Liberalism is, in short, very conservative, as we understand liberal and conservative politics today. The role of the states is to perform the limited number of tasks that individuals cannot perform by themselves, such as establishment of a basic legal system, assurance of national defense, and coining money.

The liberal view of human nature shows up an Adam Smith's writings. He believed in the cooperative, constructive side of human nature, and gave it the famous name, the "invisible hand."

> He generally, indeed, neither intends to promote the public interest, nor knows how much he is promoting it. By preferring the support of domestic to that of foreign industry, he intends only his own security; and by directing that industry in such a manner as its own produce may be of the greatest value, he intends only his own gain, and he is in this, as in many cases, led by an invisible hand to promote an end which was no part of his intention. Nor is it always the worse for the society that it was no part of it. By pursuing his own interest he frequently promotes that of society more effectually than when he really intends to promote it. I have never known much good done by those who affected to trade for the public good.[5]

It is clear that Smith sees people working in harmony, even when they are competing for the same customers or products. For the most part, then, the Smith's liberal philosophy sees no need for the heavy hand of the state in individual and market activities. Indeed, Smith was suspicious of the motives and methods of those who would use state power in the "public interest."

Some writhers paint Adam Smith as unrealistic in his optimistic view of human nature, but he was no romantic Pollyanna. Smith knew that any individual or group that gains power also gains the potential to abuse it. This is true even in the market. Smith wrote that "People of the same trade seldom meet together, even for merriment and division, but the conversation ends in a conspiracy against the public, or in some contrivance to raise prices."[6]

Adam Smith has been quoted frequently in these pages; it would be hard to overstate the importance of his writings and his ideas in the development of political economy. Smith's works struck the right note at the right time, and so gained a measure of respect and influence that is rare. It is important however, to think of both sides of Smith's writings when considering the liberal view. It is not so much that liberals such as Adam Smith love wealth, perhaps, it is more that they fear and loathe power. The fact that a liberal looks favorably on the market, where power tends to be widely dispersed, and unfavorably on the state's concentrated power, simply reflects this point of view.[7]

Section 2　Keynesian and Hegemonic Stability

(1) Keynes

John Maynard Keynes (1883-1946) developed an interesting and subtle train of the liberal perspective that we call Keynesian economics or perhaps Keynesian political economy. The Keynesian version of liberalism combines state and market influence in a way that, while still in the spirit of Adam Smith, relies on the "invisible hand" for a narrower range of issues and sees a larger, but still limited, sphere of constructive state action.

Keynes's political economy was shaped by his experiences with three of the defining events of the twentieth century: World War I, the rise of the Marxist-Leninist Soviet Union, and the world wide Great Depression of the 1930s. From World War I, Keynes learned the dangers of undiluted mercantilism. The Great War and its unstable aftermath were, in his view, the result of nationalism, greed, and vengeance.

Keynes's experiences in and with the Soviet Union discouraged any thought he might have had of adopting a Marxist or communist point of view. Keynes viewed Leninism as a religion, with a strong emotional appeal that capitalism lacked, not a theory of political economy. He found the Soviet regime repressive, its disregard for individual freedom intolerable.

Having rejected mercantilism, like Adam Smith, and communism, like Vaclav Havel, it might appear that Maynard Keynes would necessarily be a liberal. But Keynes was critical, too, of the cult of the market that extreme liberalism represents. Here he was influenced by the Great Depression of the 1930s, which he interpreted as evidence that the "invisible hand" sometimes errs in catastrophic ways. As early as 1926, Keynes wrote:

> Let us clear from the ground the metaphysical or general principles upon which, from time to time, *laissez-faire* has been founded. It is not true that individuals possess a

> prescriptive "Natural Liberty" in their economic activities. There is no "compact" conferring perpetual rights on those who have or on those who acquire. The world is not so governed from above that private and social interest always coincides. It is not a correct deduction from the Principles of Economics that enlightened self interest always operates in the public interest. Nor is it true that self-interest generally is enlightened; more often individuals acting separately to promote their own ends are too ignorant or too weak to attain even these. Experience does not show that individuals, which they make up a social unit, are always less clear-sighted than when they act separately.[8]

In Keynes's view, individuals and markets tended to make decisions that were particularly unwise when faced with situations where the future is unknown and there is no effective way to share risks or coordinate otherwise chaotic actions. Here Keynes seems to foresee the Great Depression that came just a few years later.

> Many of the greatest economic evils of our time are the fruits of risk, uncertainly, and ignorance.... Yet the cure lies outside the operations of individuals; it may even be to the interest of individuals to aggravate the disease.... These measures would involve Society in exercising directive intelligence through some appropriate organ of action over many of the inner intricacies of private business, yet it would leave private initiative and enterprise unhindered.[9]

In other words, Keynes thought that the state could use its power to fortify and improve the market, but not along the aggressive, nationalistic lines of mercantilism, and not with the oppressive force of communism. Keynes was, at heart, still a liberal, who believed in the positive force of the market.

> These reflections have been directed towards possible improvements in the technique of modern Capitalism by the agency of collective action. There is nothing in them which is seriously incompatible with what seems to me to be the essential characteristic of Capitalism, namely the dependence upon the intense appeal to the money-making and money-loving instincts of individuals as the main motive force of the economic machine.[10]
>
> For my part, I think that Capitalism, wisely managed, can probably be made more efficient for attaining economic ends than any alternative system yet in sight, but that in itself is in many ways objectionable. Our problem is to work out notions of a satisfactory way of life.[11]

Keynes's perspective on International Political Economy (IPE) finds strengths and weaknesses in both state and market. While he advanced free markets in a wide domain, including international trade and finance, for the most part, he still believed that positive government action was both useful and necessary to deal with problems that the "invisible hand" would not set right. These problems included especially the macroeconomic diseases of inflation and unemployment.

Keynes doubted that markets could fully coordinate the actions of individuals to achieve their best interests. During the Great Depression, for example, people were uncertain and afraid and tended to hold on to their money, neither spending it nor banking it. This might have been wise for them individually, but with millions of people behaving this way, the flow of spending that supports jobs and creates incomes diminished, creating unemployment, and generating more fear and uncertainty. The "paradox of saving" is that it is good for families but, taken to the extreme, it can be bad for the economy. The "invisible hand" loses its grip.

Keynes also doubted that people are invariably rational in their behavior. The stock market, he said, was influenced by the "animal spirits" of traders. The stock market crash of 1929 showed what can happen when investors are spooked and stampede.

Keynes developed a new and somewhat complex strain of IPE that was liberal on the international front but recognized a need for firm stake action internally, to overcome the obstacles of risk, uncertainty, and ignorance. Keynes's ideas formed and shaped many modern institutions, ranging from the system of international trade and finance, on one hand, to the programs of unemployment insurance, social security, and deposit insurance on the other.

(2) Hegemonic stability

The theory of hegemonic stability is another variation on the liberal theme, different from Keynes but clearly reflecting the Keynesian spirit. This theory looks at the role of state and market in the global economy and observes that international markets work best when certain international public goods[12] are present. These public goods include such things as free trade, peace and security, or at least a balance of powers, and a sound system of international payments.

Each of these public goods is costly to provide, and each suffers from what economists call the "free-rider problem". Individuals and nations who do not contribute to the cost of providing these public goods will still be able to benefit from them. Under these circumstances, it will often be the case that the world economy will suffer, since no nation will be willing to bear all the costs of enforcing free trade, sound money, and so on, while others derive benefits without paying. At certain times, however, there emerges one nation that dominates the world economy. That nation finds it in its own interest to provide international public goods, even taking free riders into account. The hegemon benefits so much from the growth and success of the world economy that it is willing to bear the costs of providing international public goods to smaller or weaker states, who find it in their interest to cooperate in order to preserve their "free ride."

The liberal theory of hegemonic stability asserts that, when a hegemon arises, the world economy tends to grow and prosper, as the benefits of free trade, peace and security, sound money, etc., stimulate markets everywhere. When the hegemon fails, however, these public goods disappear and the world economy stagnates or declines. Political economists generally recognize three instance of hegemonic stability in modern history: The United Provinces (Holland) was the hegemon in the eighteenth century, Great Britain was the hegemon in the nineteenth century, and the United States performed the hegemon's function for much of the postwar era.

The hegemonic stability theory has stimulated a great deal of discussion. Scholars ask, what happens when there is no hegemon? Is the U.S. still a hegemon? If the U.S. is a "hegemon in decline", then is some sort of group hegemon possible, involving the European Union or perhaps a U.S.-Japan "bigemony"?

Scholars also debate the motives and effects of hegemony. Is the hegemon unselfish, draining itself dry in the end as it tries to keep the international system running? Or is the hegemon selfish and imperialistic, draining the rest of the world to fill its coffers?

Like the Keynesian viewpoint, the liberal theory of hegemonic stability is based on the strength and resiliency of the market as a form of social and economic organization. Whereas Keynes thought that the state needed to be active within nations, to assure economic growth and stability, the hegemonic stability theory asserts that one state—the hegemon—needs to shoulder an international role if markets are to achieve their potential. Where Keynes called for domestic policy, the hegemonic stability focuses on international policies.

Section 3 The Politics of International Regimes

All economists and political economists acknowledge the need for some minimal rules or institutions to govern and regulate economic activities; even the most ardent public -choice economist would agree that laws are needed to enforce contracts and protect property rights. A liberal international economy certainly needs agreed-upon rules. A liberal economy can succeed only if it provides public goods like a stable monetary system, eliminates market failures, and prevents cheating and free-riding. Although the primary purpose of rules or regimes is to resolve economic problems, many are actually enacted for political rather than for strictly economic reasons. For example, although economists may be correct that an economy benefits from opening itself to free trade whether or not other countries open their own markets to it, a liberal international economy could not politically tolerate too many free-riders who benefit from the opening of other economies, but refuse to open their own markets.

In the past, the rules governing international economy were quite simple and informal. Insofar as the implicit rules were enforced at all, they were enforced by the major powers whose interests were favored by those rules. For example, in the nineteenth century under the Pax Britannica, overseas property rights were frequently upheld by British "gunboat diplomacy,"[13] and the international gold standard, based on a few generally accepted rules, was managed by the Bank of England. Now, formal international institutions have been created to manage today's extraordinarily complex international economy. The most important institutions are the Bretton Woods institutions such as the World Bank, the International Monetary Fund, and the World Trade Organization. The world economy would have difficulty functioning without these institutions. Therefore, understanding their functioning has become an extremely important concern of political economists.

The concept of international regimes, defined as "sets of implicit or explicit principles, norms, rules, and decision-making procedures around which actor's expectations converge in a given area of international relations," has been at the core of the research on international institutions. Although a distinction can be made between an international regime as rules and understandings and an international institution as a formal organization, the word "regimes" and the word "institutions" are frequently used interchangeably in writings on international political economy. Moreover, what is really important for the functioning of the world economy are the rules themselves rather than the formal institutions in which they are usually embodied. To simplify the following discussion, I shall use "international organizations as the International Monetary Fund or the General Agreement on Tariffs and Trade."

Robert Keohane has been the most influential scholar in the development of regime theory. In his book, *After Hegemony* (1984), Keohane set forth the definitive exposition and classic defense of regime theory.[14] He argues that international regimes are a necessary feature of the world economy and are required to facilitate efficient operation of the international economy. Among the tasks performed by regimes are reduction of uncertainty, minimization of transaction cost, and prevention of market failures. International regimes are created by self-centered states in order to further both individual and collective interest. Even though a particular regime might be created because of the pressures of a dominant power (or hegemon), Keohane argues that an effective international regime takes on a life of its own over time. Moreover, when states experience the success of an international regime, they "learn" to change their own behavior and even to redefine their national interests. Thus, according to Keohane's analysis, international regimes are necessary to preserve and stabilize the international economy.

From its beginning, regime theory has been surrounded by intense controversy. One major reason for the intensity of this debate is that regime theory arose as a response to what Keohane labeled "the theory of hegemonic stability."[15] Proponents of the latter theory had argued that the post war liberal international economy was based on the economic and political leadership of the United States. Some theorists had argued that the hegemonic stability theory also suggested that the relative decline of American power due to the rise of new economic powers and the slowing of American productivity growth in the early 1970s placed the continued existence of a liberal world economy in jeopardy. Keohane and others argued that international regimes and cooperation among the major economic powers would replace declining American leadership as the basis of the liberal international economic order. Thus, the political purpose of regime theory was, at least in part, to reassure American and others that a liberal international order would survive American's economic decline and the severe economic problems of the 1970s.

British scholar Susan Strange was the most outspoken critic of regime theory.[16] According to Strange, regime theory was at best a passing fad, and at worst a polemical device designed to legitimate American's continuing domination of the world economy. Strange and other critics alleged that such international regimes as those governing trade and monetary affairs had been economically, politically, and ideologically biased in America's favor, and that these regimes were put in place by American power, reflected American interests, and were not (as American regime theorists have argued) politically and economically neutral. Strange charged that many of the fundamental problems afflicting the world economy actually resulted from ill-conceived and predatory American economic policies rather than simply being symptoms of American economic decline.

Strange's foremost example of American culpability was the huge American demand in the 1980s and 1990s for international capital to finance America's federal budget and trade/payments deficit.[17] Through use of what she referred to as "structural power" (such as America's military, financial, and technological power), she alleged that United States continued to run the world economy during that period and made a mess of it. Strange and other critics also alleged that the role of the dollar as the key international currency had permitted the United States to behave irresponsibly. More generally, Strange and other foreign critics charged that the American discipline of international political economy, and regime theory in particular, have been little more than efforts to defend American's continuing desire to reign economically and politically over the rest of the world. Whether or not we accept these criticisms, they should remind us that regimes and other social institutions are sometimes created to preserve inequalities as well as to improve coordination and overcome other obstacles to mutually beneficial cooperation.[18]

Section 4　Marxism, Dependency and World System Theory

(1) Marx and History

Karl Marx (1818-1883) understood history to be a great, dynamic, evolving creature, determined fundamentally by economic and technological forces. Marx believed that through a process called historical materialism these forces can be objectively explained and understood just like any other natural law.

Historical materialism takes as its starting point the nation that the forces of production of society set the parameters for the kind of system of political economy, or mode of production, that is possible. As Marx put it, "the hand mill gives you society with the feudal lord, the steam mill society with the industrial capitalist."[19] The economic structure (what Marx Called the relations of production, or class relations) that emerges from such a mode of production in turn determines the social and ethical structures of society.

It is in the contradictions or conflicts between the forces of production and the relations of production in a society that Marx sees the mechanism for evolutionary and revolutionary change. Marx sees the course of history as steadily evolving. The process of change from one system of political economy (or mode of production, in Marx's words) to another is rooted in the growing contradiction between the forces of production (technological development) and the class or property relations in which they develop.

Since class relations change more slowly than technological development, social change is impeded, fostering conflict between the classes. An example today would be computers, which open up possibilities of different class relations and more free time for workers. But because capitalists control how technology is used, many of the computer's potential gains are not realized. When that conflict becomes so severe as to block the advance of human development, a social revolution sweeps away the existing legal and political arrangements and replaces them with ones more compatible with continued social progress.

In this way, history has evolved through distinct epochs or stages: primitive communism, slavery, feudalism, capitalism, socialism, and finally arrival at pure communism. In each of these modes of production, there is a dialectical process whereby inherently unstable and tortured opposing economic forces and counter forces lead to crisis, revolution, and to the next stage of history. And for Marx, the agents of that change are human beings organized in conflicting social classes.

(2) Modern World System Theory

The structuralist perspective has very variants in the modern world. These different viewpoints share the basic idea that the structure of the global economy strongly influences the IPE. Beyond this, they differ in many important ways.

One fascinating contemporary variant of the structuralist perspective focuses on the way in which the global system has developed since the middle of the fifteenth century. This is the Modern World System (MWS) Theory[20] originated by Immanuel Wallerstein and developed by a number of scholars, including Christopher Chase Dunn. Capitalist in nature, the world system largely determines political and social relations, both within and between nations and other international entities.

For Wallerstein, the world economy provides the sole means of organization in the international system. The modern world system exhibits the following characteristics: a single division of labor whereby nation-states are mutually dependent upon economic exchange; the sale of products and goods for the sake of profit; and, finally, the division of the world into three functional areas or socioeconomic units, which correspond to the role nations within these regions play in the international economy.

From the MWS perspective the capitalist core states of northwest Europe in the sixteenth century moved beyond agricultural specialization to higher-skilled industries modes of production by penetrating and absorbing other regions into the capitalist world economy. Through this process, Eastern Europe became the agricultural *periphery* and exported grains, bullion, wood, cotton, and sugar to the core. Mediterranean Europe and its labor-intensive industries became the *semi-periphery* or intermediary between the core and periphery.

It would be easy to define the core, periphery and semi-periphery in terms of the types of nations within each group (such as the U.S., China, and Korea, respectively), but the MWS is not based primarily on the nation-state. In this theory, the core represents a geographic region made up of nation-states that play a partial role in the modern world system. The force of bourgeoisie interests actually exists, in varying degrees, in every country. Every nation has elements of core, periphery, and semi-periphery, although not equally so. In common with Marx, then, the MWS theory looks at IPE in terms of class relations and patterns of exploitation.

According to Wallerstein, the core states dominate the peripheral states through unequal exchange for the purpose of extracting cheap raw materials instead of, as Lenin argued, merely using the periphery as a market for dumping surplus production. The core interacts with the semi-periphery and periphery through the global structure of capitalism, exploiting these regions but also transforming them. The semi-periphery serves more of a political than an economic role; it is both exploited and exploiter, diffusing opposition of the periphery to the core region.

Interestingly, on some issues, Wallerstein attempts to bridge mercantilism (and political realism) with Marxist views about the relationship of politics to economics. For instance, as a mercantilist would, he accept the notion that the world is politically arranged in an anarchical manner, i.e., there is no single sovereign political authority to govern interstate relations. However, much like a Marxist-Leninist, he proposes that power politics and social differences are also conditioned by the capitalist structure of the world economy.

According to Wallerstein, capitalism within core nation-state authority acts as an instrument to maximize individual profit. Historically, the state served economic interests to the extent that "state machineries of the core states were strengthened to meet the needs of capitalist land owners and their merchant allies."[21] Wallerstein also argues that "once created," state machineries, have a certain amount of autonomy.[22] On the other hand, politics is constrained by economic structure. He asserts, for instance, that strong (core) states dominate weak (peripheral) ones because placement of the nation-state in the world capital system affects its ability to influence its global role. As Wallerstein puts it; "The functioning then of a capitalist world-economy requires that groups pursue their economic interests within a single world market while seeking to distort this market for their benefit by organizing to exert influence on states, some of which are far more powerful than others but none of which controls the world-market in its entirety."[23]

Wallerstein's conception of the modern world system has gained a good deal of notoriety in the last twenty years. He offers us a recipe of ideas and concepts that are relatively easy to understand and that account for a large part of the relationship of Northern developed to Southern developing nations. "Semi-periphery" also seems to fit the status of the newly industrialized countries (NICs). Furthermore, the MWS approach to structuralism sees exploitation as an inherent element of the capitalist structures both within and among core, periphery, and semi-periphery.

One thing that is problematic about Wallerstein's views is precisely what makes them so attractive: his comprehensive yet almost simple way of characterizing IPE. Many criticize his theory for being too deterministic, both economically and in terms of the constraining effects of the global capitalist system. Nation-states are not free to choose courses of action or policies. Instead, they are relegated to playing economically determined roles. Finally, Wallerstein is faulted for viewing capitalism as the end-product of current history.

(3) Dependency Theory

Another contemporary variant of the structuralist perspective is called *Dependency Theory*. A wide range of views can be grouped together under this heading. Their differences, however, are less important to us here than what they have in common, which is the view that the structure of the global political economy essentially enslaves the less developed countries of the "South" by making them dependent on the nations of the capitalist core of the "North."[24] Theotonio Dos Santos has written:

> By dependence we mean a situation in which the economy of certain countries is conditioned by the development and expansion of another economy to which the former is subjected. The relation of interdependence between two or more economics, and between these and world trade, assumes the form of dependence when some countries (the dominant ones) can expand and can be self-sustaining, while others (the dependent ones) can do this only as a reflection of that expansion, which can have either a positive or a negative effect on their immediate development.[25]

Dos Santos sees three eras of dependence in modern history: colonial dependence (during the eighteenth and nineteenth centuries), financial-industrial dependence (during the nineteenth and early twentieth centuries), and a structure of dependence today based on the postwar multinational corporations.

One dependency theorist in particular has focused a good deal of attention on the effects of imperialism is Latin America. Andre Gunder Frank rejects the Marxist notion that societies go through different stages or modes of production as they develop. However, he supports the imperialism thesis that connections between developed and developing regions of the world resulted in exploitation of peripheral regions by metropolitan capitalist countries.

Frank is noted for his "development of underdevelopment" thesis. He argues that developing nations never were "underdeveloped" in the sense that one might think of them as "backward" or traditional societies. Instead, once great civilizations in their own right, the developing regions of the world became underdeveloped as a result of their colonization by the Western industrialized nations. Along with exploitation, imperialism produced underdevelopment. "historical research demonstrates that contemporary underdevelopment is in large part the historical product of past and continuing economic and other relations between the satellite underdeveloped and the now developed metropolitan countries."[26]

How are developing nations to develop if in fact they are exploited by the developed capitalist industrial powers? Dependency theorists have suggested a variety of responses to this trap. A number of researchers—for example, Andre Gunder Frank—have called for peripheral nations to with draw from the global political economy. In the 1950s and 1960s, the leadership of many socialist movements in the third world favored revolutionary tactics and ideological mass movements to change not only the fundamental dynamic of both the political and economic order of their society, but also the world capitalist system.

More recently, dependency theorists have recommended a variety of other strategies and policies by which developing nations could industrialize and develop. Raul Prebisch, an Argentinean economist, was instrumental in founding, under the auspices of the United Nations, the United Nations Committee on Trade and Development (UNCTAD). The developing nations who have joined this body within the UN have made it their goal to monitor and recommend policies that would, in effect, help redistribute power and income between Northern developed and Southern developing countries. These and other dependency theorists, however, have been more aggressive about reforming the international economy and have supported the calls for a New International Economic Order (NIEO) which gained momentum shortly after the OPEC oil price hike in 1973.

The important point to make here is that dependency theories have served as part of a critique of the relationship of the metropolitan to satellite, or core to peripheral, nations. Whether or not that relationship can be equalized is a matter developed elsewhere. These theories are important to this thesis.

(1) The classic definition of the state is Max Weber's, which emphasizes its administrative and legal qualities. See Max Weber, *The Theory of Social and Economic Organization* (New York: The Free Press, 1947), p.156.

(2) In oversimplified terms, the "price-specie flow mechanism" states that the flow of specie (gold or silver) into an economy as a consequence of trade/payments surplus increases the domestic money supply and raises prices of a country's exports. This price rise in turn decreases the country's trade/payments surplus. In short, any attempt to have a permanent trade/payments surplus is self-defeating.

(3) Joseph M. Grieco, *Cooperation Among Nations: Europe, America, and Non-Tariff Barriers to Trade* (Ithaca: Cornell University Press, 1990). An excellent volume on the debate over the importance of relative versus absolute gains is David A. Baldwin, ed., *Neorealism and Neoliberalism: The Contemporary Debate* (New York: Columbia University Press, 1993).

(4) Ralf Dahrendorf, "Liberalism," in John Eatwell, Murray Milgate, and Peter Newman, eds., *The New Palgrave: Invisible Hand* (New York: W.W. Norton, 1989), p.183.

(5) Adam Smith, *The wealth of Nations* (New York: Dutton, 1964), p.401

(6) Ibid., 117

(7) To Smith, the "state" meant Britain's Parliament, which represented the interest of the landed

gentry, not the entrepreneurs and citizens of the growing industrial centers. Not until the 1830s was Parliament reformed to distribute political power more widely. As a Scot without landed estates, Smith had some reason to question the power structure of his time.

(8) John Maynard Keynes, "The End of Laissez-Faire," in *Essays in Persuasion* (New York: W. W. Norton, 1963), p. 312

(9) Ibid. p.208.

(10) Ibid. p.319.

(11) Ibid. p.321.

(12) In non-technical language, a public or collective good is one that everyone can enjoy without having to pay for the use of the good. A frequently used example is a lighthouse. Because of this free use, no one usually has an incentive to provide them and therefore public goods tend to be "underprovided." The literature on this subject and on proposed solutions to the underprovision problem is extensive.

(13) Charles Lipson, *Standing Guard: Protecting Foreign Capital in the Nineteenth and Twentieth Centuries* (Berkeley: University of California Press, 1985)

(14) Robert O. Keohane, *After Hegemony: Cooperation and Discord in the World Political Economy* (Princeton: Princeton University Press, 1984).

(15) Robert O. Keohane, "The Theory of Hegemonic Stability and Changes in International Economic Regimes, 1967-1977," in Ole Holsti et al., *Change in the International System* (Boulder, Colo.: Westview Press, 1980): p.131-62

(16) Susan Strange, "Cave! hic Dragones: A Critique of Regime Analysis," in Stephen D. Krasner, ed., *International Regimes*, p.337-54.

(17) Susan Strange, *Casino Capitalism* (New York: Basil Blackwell, 1986); and Susan Strange, *Mad Money* (Manchester, U.K.: Manchester University Press, 1998).

(18) Andrew Schotter, *The Economic Theory of Social Institutions* (New York: Cambridge University Press, 1981), p.26.

(19) Karl Marx, *The Poverty of Philosophy* (New York: International Publishers, 1963), p.122.

(20) Immanuel Wallerstein, The Rise and Future Demise of the World Capitalist System: Concepts for Comparative Analysis, *Comparative Studies in Society and History*, 16 (September 1974): p. 387-415

(21) Ibid., p.402

(22) Ibid.,

(23) Ibid., p.406

(24) Dependency theory is thus seen as an interpretation of North-South IPE relations.

(25) Theotonio Dos Santos, "The Structure of Dependence," *American Economic Review* 60 (1970): p.231-236

(26) Andre Gunder Frank, *Capitalism and Underdevelopment in Latin America: Historical Studies of Chile and Brazil* (New York: Monthly Review Press, 1967), p.9.

Chapter 3 The rise of Globalization

Section 1 The changing of world economic order

　The most important change has been the end of Cold War and of the Soviet threat to the United States and its European and Japanese allies. Throughout most of the last half of the twentieth century, the Cold War and its alliance structures provided the framework within which the world economy functioned. The United States and its major allies generally subordinated potential economic conflicts to the need to maintain political and security cooperation. Emphasis on security interests and alliance cohesion provided the political glue that held the world economy together and facilitated compromises of important national differences over economic issues. With the end of the Cold War, American leadership and the close economic cooperation among the capitalist powers waned. Simultaneously, the market-oriented world grew much larger as formerly communist and Third World countries became more willing to participate in the market system; this has been exemplified by the much more active role taken by the less developed countries (LDCs) in the World Trade Organization (WTO). While this development is to be welcomed, it has made the task of managing the global economic system more daunting.

　Economic globalization has entailed a few key developments in trade, finance, and foreign direct investment by multinational corporations. International trade in services (banking, information, etc.) has also significantly increased. With the decreasing cost of transportation, more and more goods are becoming "tradeables." With the immense expansion of world trade, international competition has greatly increased. Openness, many businesses find themselves competing against foreign firms that have improved their efficiency. During the 1980s and 1990s, trade competition became even more intense as a growing number of industrializing economies in East Asia and elsewhere shifted from an import substitution to an exported growth strategy. Nevertheless, the major competitors for almost all American firms remain other American firms.

　Underlying the expansion of global trade has been a number of developments. Since World War Ⅱ, trade barriers have declined significantly due to successive rounds of trade negotiations. During the last half of the twentieth century average tariff levels of the United States and other industrialized countries dropped from about 40 percent to only 6 percent, and barriers to trade in services have also been lowered.[1] In addition, from the late 1970s onward, deregulation and privatization further opened national economies to imports. Technological advances in communications and reduced transportation costs have significantly encouraged trade expansion. Taking advantage of these economic and technological changes, more and more businesses have participated in international markets. Nevertheless, despite these developments, most trade takes place among the three advanced industrial economies—the United States, Western Europe, and Japan, plus a few emerging markets in East Asia, Latin America, and elsewhere. Most of the less developed world is excluded, except as exporters of food and raw materials. It is estimated, for example, that Africa South of the Sahara accounted for only about 1 percent of total world trade in the 1990s.

Since the mid-1970s, financial deregulation and the creation of new financial instruments, such as derivatives, and technological advances in communications have contributed to a much more highly integrated international financial system. The volume of foreign exchange trading (buying and selling national currencies) in the late 1990s reached approximately $1.5 trillion per day, an eightfold increase since 1986. The significance of these huge investments is greatly magnified by the fact that a large portion of foreign investments is leveraged; that is, they are investment made with borrowed funds. Finally, derivatives or repackaged securities and other financial assets play an important role in international finance. Valued (by BIS) at $360 trillion (larger than the value of the entire global economy), they have contributed to the complexity and the instability of international finance. It is obvious that international finance has a profound impact on the global economy.

This financial revolution has linked national economies much more closely to one another and has also increased the capital available for developing countries. As many of these financial flows are short-term, highly volatile, and speculative, international finance has become the most unstable aspect of the global capitalist economy. The immense scale, velocity, and speculative nature of financial movements across national borders have made governments more vulnerable to sudden shifts in these movements. Governments can therefore easily fall prey to currency speculators, as happened in the 1992 European financial crisis, which caused Great Britain to withdraw from the European Exchange Rate Mechanism, and in the 1994-95 punishing collapse of the Mexican peso, as well as in the devastating East Asian financial crisis in the late 1990s. Whereas, for some, financial globalization exemplifies the healthy and beneficial triumph of global capitalism, for others the international financial system is "out of control" and must be better regulated. Either way, international finance is the one area wherein the term "globalization" is most appropriately applied.

The term "globalization" came into popular usage in the second half of the 1980s in connection with the huge surge of foreign direct investment (FDI) by multinational corporations (MNCs). MNCs and FDI have been around for several centuries in the form of the

East India Company and other "merchant adventures." In the early postwar decades, most FDI was made by American firms, and the United States was host to only a small amount of FDI from non-American firms. Then, in the 1980s, FDI expanded significantly and much more rapidly than world trade and global economic output. In the early post war decades, Japanese, West European, and other nationalities became major investors and the United States became both the world's largest home and host economy. As a consequence of these developments, FDI outflows from the major industrialized countries to the industrializing countries rose to approximately 15 percent annually. The largest fraction of FDI amounts to hundreds of billions of dollars. The greatest portion of this investment has been in services and especially in high-tech industries such as automobiles and information technology. Information, in fact, has itself became a "tradeable," and this raises such new issues in international commerce as the protection of intellectual property rights and market access for service industries. In combination with increased trade and financial flows, the increasing importance of MNCs has significantly transformed the international economy.

Although the end of the Cold War provided the necessary political condition for the creation of a truly global economy, it is economic, political, and technological developments that have been the driving force behind economic globalization. Novel technologies in transportation have caused the costs of transportation, especially transoceanic travel, to fall greatly, thus opening the possibility of a global trading system. In addition, the computer and advances in telecommunications have greatly increased global financial flows. These developments have been extremely important in enabling multinational firms to pursue global economic strategies and operations. The compression of time and space resulting from these technological changes has significantly reduced the costs of international commerce. Globalization has also been produced by international economic cooperation and new economic policies. Under American leadership, both the industrialized and industrializing economies have taken a number of initiatives to lower trade and investment barriers. Eight rounds of multilateral trade negotiations under the General Agreement on Tariffs and Trade (GATT), the principal forum for trade liberalization, have significantly decreased trade barriers. In addition, more and more nations have been pursuing neo-liberal economic policies such as deregulation and privatization. These developments have resulted in an increasingly market-oriented global economy.

Many observers believe that a profound shift is taking place from a state-dominated to a market-dominated international economy. Humanity, many argue, is moving rapidly toward a politically borderless world. The collapse of the Soviet command economy, the failure of the Third World's import-substitution strategy, and the outstanding economic success of the American economy in the 1990s have encouraged acceptance of unrestricted markets as the solution to the economic ills of modern society. As deregulation and other reforms have reduced the role of the state in the economy, many believe that markets have become the most important mechanism for determining both domestic and international economic and even political affairs. In a highly integrated global economy, the nation-state, according to this interpretation, has become an anachronism and is in retreat. Many also believe that the decline of the state is leading to an open and truly global capitalist economy characterized by unrestricted trade, financial flows, and the international activities of multinational firms.

Although most economists and many others welcome this development, critics emphasize the "high costs" of economic globalization, including growing income inequality both among and within nations, high chronic levels of unemployment in Western Europe and elsewhere, and, most of all, environmental degradation, widespread exploitation, and the devastating consequences for national economies wrought by unregulated international financial flows. These critics charge that national societies are being integrated into a global economic system and are buffeted by economic and technological forces over which they have little or no control. They view global economic problems as proof that the costs of globalization are much greater than its benefits. Foreseeing a world characterized by intense economic conflict at both the domestic and international levels, and believing that an open world economy will inevitably produce more losers than winners, critics argue that unleashing market and other economic forces has caused an intense struggle among individual nations, economic classes, and powerful groups. Many assert that what former German Chancellor Helmut Schmit called "the struggle for the world product" could result in competing regional blocs dominated by one or another of the major economic powers.

The idea that globalization is responsible for most of the world's economic, political, and other problems is either patently false or greatly exaggerated. In fact, other factors such as technological developments and imprudent national policies are much more important than globalization as causes of many, if not most, of the problems for which globalization is held responsible. Unfortunately, misunderstandings regarding globalization and its effects have contributed to growing disillusionment with borders open to trade and investment, and have led to the belief that globalization has had a very negative impact on workers, the environment, and less developed countries. According to an American poll taken in April 1999, 52 percent of the respondents had negative views regarding globalization.[2] Yet, even though globalization is an important feature of the international economy that has changed many aspects of the subject of international political economy, the fact is that globalization is not as pervasive, extensive, or significant as many would have believe. Most national economies are still mainly self-contained rather than globalized; globalization is also restricted to a limited, albeit rapidly increasing, number of economic sectors. Moreover, globalization is largely restricted to the triad of industrialized countries and to the emerging markets of East Asia. Most importantly, many of the attacks on globalization by its critics are misplaced; many of its "evils" are really due to changes that have little or nothing to do with globalization.

The end of the Cold War and the growth of economic globalization coincided with a new industrial revolution based on the computer and the rise of the Information or Internet Economy. Technological developments are transforming almost every aspect of economic, political, and social affairs as computing power provides an impetus to the world economy that may prove as significant as those previously produced by steam power, electric power, and oil power. The economics profession, however, has been deeply divided about whether or not computing power represents a technological revolution on the same scale as these earlier advances. Although the computer appears to have accelerated the rate of economic and productivity growth, it is still too early to know whether or not its ultimate impact will affect the overall economy on a scale at all equivalent to that produced by the dynamo. A growing number of economists, however, believe that computers have an important impact not only on productivity, but also on economic affairs in general. For example, some economists believe that the organization of and the ways in which national economies function are experiencing major changes in response to the computer and the Internet. Although it is still much too early to gauge the full impact of the computer on the economy, it is certain that the computer and the Information Economy are significantly changing many aspects of economic affairs. Most importantly, in the industrialized countries, they have accelerated the shift from manufacturing to services. This pervasive economic restructuring of the industrialized economies is economically costly and politically difficult.

During the last decades of the twentieth century, there was a significant shift in the distribution of world industry away from the older industrial economies toward Pacific Asia, Latin America, and other rapidly industrializing economies. Although the United States and the other industrialized economies still possess a preponderant share of global wealth and industry, they have declined in relative terms, while the industrializing economies, especially China, have gained economic importance. Before the 1997 financial crisis, which began in Thailand and eventually plunged East Asia into political and economic turmoil, Pacific Asia's economic success had been extremely impressive. Many of these economies achieved average annual growth rates of 6 to 8 percent. And despite the financial crisis, such economic "fundamentals" as high savings rates and excellent workforces support the belief that these emerging markets will continue to be important actors in the global economy.

Section 2　The Benefits and Critics of Globalization

(1) **Benefits**

　Behind globalization lies considerably more than a hope and a prayer and a burst of new technology; it is the product of a solid edifice of economic theory and the practical lessons of economic history. Arguments for free trade have been advancing for 2,500 years and have held the intellectual high ground for most of the last two centuries.

　A contemporary statement of the economic benefits of globalization would draw first on various strands of theory: traditional trade theory illustrating the efficiency gains from specialization between countries with different resource endowments, the benefits of economies of scale on an international level[3], the stimulus to efficiency from increased competition, the benefits of trade creation, scale and competition within regional groups, and the costs of protection in the form of rent-seeking behaviour. To these would be added the arguments for achieving benefits of specialization, scale and competition through direct investment flows as well as trade and the spread of technology and 'best practice' through multinational companies. The adoption of these arguments by UNCTAD has been an important change in the intellectual climate. A more contemporary and controversial case has been made for globally free capital markets on grounds of efficiency and competition. All of this work supports the notion that there is potential benefit from open rather than closed economies.

　A crucially important additional strand of support has come from contemporary welfare economics, deriving from the Theory of the Second Best which is specifically directed to the problems faced by activist modern governments anxious to deal with environmental failures, inequality, and other social ills. This shows that these objectives will invariably not discriminate against foreigners, such as on imports, inward investment or immigrants.

　The structure of supporting theory would mean little if it were not reflected in economic reality. The enduring support (with, of course, many specific exceptions) for liberal economic policies and international integration derives credibility from the following factors: the historical, and contemporary, experience of rapid economic growth associated with rapid trade growth; the negative experiences of periods of protectionism and of 'rent-seeking' behaviour; the contract between export-led development in East Asia and southern Europe and inward-looking development in Latin America; the failure and pathological excesses of autarky in North Korea, Cambodia, or Burma; and the wider failure of the socialist system of the USSR and COMECON, largely isolated from international capitalism.

　A further factor is the ability of countries to demonstrate the advantages of virtually complete economic openness, and to embrace globalization while achieving a high level of political commitment to equality and income distribution, universal services, environmental protection and workers' rights. Some of the more successful emerging economies have also managed to reconcile growth with low levels of inequality.

(2) The critics

Globalization has its critics; there are essentially three strands which can be separated out. The first, and most fundamental, is an extension of the Marxist-Leninist critique of capitalism to the world economy: the idea that international economic integration is an inherent part of a process of exploitation of labor and of weak commodity-producing countries. The arguments have been updated mostly in the context of the post-colonial debate on development and were very influential in the 1960s in encouraging ideas of 'de-linkage' and 'self-reliance', free from 'dependency' on Western-dominated international capitalism. They still provide a conscious, or unconscious, underpinning for a number of contemporary arguments despite the failure of alternative models of development based on Marxist ideology, or 'self-reliance'.

A second strand is less radical and operates within an essentially neo-classical framework: identifying specific instances where mal-distribution of the gains from trade (or investment) might justify a major departure from liberal policy in respect of trade or investment.

There is the classic 'term of trade' argument advanced by Prebisch (1959) and others ― which was highly influential in the 1950s and 1960s—to justify a conscious strategy to diversify from commodity exporting to manufactures, protected from international competition. It is certainly possible to demonstrate theoretically, and with examples, that commodity-based export growth can be immiserizing if all the benefits of export expansion are passed on to importers in lower prices. And there has been in practice a long-term trend of decline in barter terms of trade for primary commodities. But one lesson from experience has been that manufactured products are a much better route to diversification than highly protected import substitutes which in Latin America and India, after an initial burst of industrial growth, proved to be inefficient and unsustainable in terms of external payments and as a cause of widening inequality. Arguments for protectionism based on protected industrialization now enjoy little credibility, but they have a lingering influence in countries such as India. A different argument is that advanced countries relatively well endowed with capital rather than labor will tend (under some rather restrictive assumptions) to see wages decline relative to other income sources when trading with labor-abundant, low-wage countries. This proposition is used to argue that rich countries may have to protect themselves against 'cheap' labor to prevent a decline in the real wages (and working conditions) of their industrial workers, particularly the unskilled. The arguments have been advanced in the political arena with varying degrees of crudity and the populist potential has been exploited recently, especially in the US and less successfully in Europe. Some impetus has been given to the debate by serious research suggesting that unskilled wages may not have grown as fast as GDP in some rich countries because of import competition (and immigration). Other empirical studies dispute the facts or, while accepting some degree of download pressure on unskilled wages from international trade competition and immigration, argue that these are relatively minor compared with the impact of technology or the wider policy environment. And most economists, even if disagreeing on the facts, would argue that trade protectionism (or curbs on direct investment) is a very poor, and understandable, way to improve wages and conditions of industrial-sector workers.

One recent addition to the set of well-worn arguments has come from so-called 'Strategic Trade Theory' which has created a new set of justifications for national governments to interpose themselves between the world economy and domestic business. In some respects, these arguments update very old 'infant industry' arguments for temporary protection based on possible externalities or other arguments for consciously turning the terms of trade against other countries (the 'optimum tariff'). But they go further to incorporate game theory to describe the interactions between small numbers of large companies and governments in such industries as aerospace, satellite communications, basic telecommunications and computer software. Much of the empirical work does not suggest that 'strategic' intervention by governments has had the positive effects it claimed and, in any event, few of the proponents of 'strategic' intervention are suggesting a whole-scale withdrawal from international economic integration as opposed to attempts to intervene in some special cases.

In addition to these well-established academic debates there is emerging a third strand: what could be called 'the new protectionism'. What is striking in the literature about some of the 'new protectionism' is that it is not, in fact, very new, and draws extensively on dependency theory and 'economic imperialism'. Also, Much of it, could not be dignified by calling it economic argument since it repudiates many of the most fundamental sources of economic advances and rising living standards (specialization; economies of scale) in favor of 'self-reliant' communities and countries.

But some of the more sophisticated texts introduce some genuinely challenging ideas. The most important concerns the pervasive nature of environmental crisis: the irrevocable loss of environmental assets such as tropical forests or fish stocks and the impact of pollution on such traditional 'sinks' as the atmosphere, the ozone layer and the oceans. The problem with this approach is that even if the pessimistic analysis of global environmental trends is valid (and this is vigorously disputed), there is no logical link between a concern for the environment and protectionist approaches to trade and investment. First of all, there is now a well-developed field of environmental economics demonstrating that environmental externalities should be dealt with by applying the 'polluter pays principle' through taxation or regulatory instruments; in no way does it justify discriminating against imports over domestic production or against foreign investment over domestic capitalists. Secondly, there is an underlying trend—intensified by the competitive pressures of globalization—towards dematerialization and more efficient resource use (one consequence of which is weakening commodity prices). Thirdly, 'self-reliance' has a bad history. The world's most serious examples of environmental degradation and wasteful resource use are in the former USSR and Northern China which developed without the discipline of markets or access to good environmental practice through foreign investment and trade. Fourthly, the link between extreme poverty and environmental stress is well established. 'Self-reliant' subsistence agriculture and nomadic practices can be immensely destructive to the natural environment in conditions of rising population, far more than multinational agribusinesses. More serious treatment of environmental sustainability has stressed the importance of international economic integration.

The one specific concern of environmentalists is that trade generates environmental pollution through cross-border transport. The point is valid as far as it goes, but is trivial in relation to the sum of environmental externalities. This could be better addressed by taxing all road and air freight traffic on the 'polluter pays principle', versus by stopping trade.

There are some unifying themes in the old and the new criticisms of globalization which represent entirely valid concerns even if they lead to wrong conclusions. One is that globalization provides for cross border capital, rather than labor, mobility and is therefore more likely to improve returns to capital rather than labor. Modern manifestations of globalization center on the rapid growth of foreign direct investment and short-term capital flows rather than trade in goods or labor movement. The appropriate answer to this asymmetry, however, is not to retreat into national or regional autarky, but to open markets to labor-intensive products and services (removing current biases against these items in tariff and other protective structures in rich countries) and to seek to extend liberalizing trade rules to labor-only services (blocked by rich countries at present).

The other worry is that the gap between rich and poor countries is widening. Few reports on the states of the world fail to point out that the distribution of income internationally is massively skewed, though there is an enormous range of estimates depending largely upon whether income per capita is measured in nominal prices and exchange rates or in purchasing power equivalents, the latter being less extreme. Maddison's work on long-term economic trends (1995) shows that the degree of divergence between 'rich' and 'poor' has grown steadily in a century and a half of modernization and growing integration, albeit in the context of generally rising absolute standards. According to the data from IMF, in 1820 the per capita incomes in pre-colonial Africa at present prices were around $450, $625 in China, and $1,135 in pre-industrial Japan. These figures are not enormously lower than those of the world's richest country at that time, Britain—with around $1,750—or the European average of around $1,225. While African and Indian incomes have roughly doubled in over a century and a half to $840 and $1,350 respectively, those of Western Europe have multiplied 14 times and those of Japan 17 times. The gap between the richest and poorest country in Maddison's sample of 56 countries has widened from a ratio of 1:3 to 1:72 (that is, between the US and Ethiopia). The period of postwar growth has widened disparities considerably overall, but has also reduced disparities between the rich and those countries that are rapidly catching up (East and Southeast Asia, and in southern Europe) while creating a new class of under-performers in Latin America and Eastern Europe. The 1980s and 1990s have produced a new crop of catch-up candidates including, notably, China.

But is globalization part of the problem or part of the solution? Disparities are undoubtedly much more evident as a result of improved communications. Extreme wealth and world poverty are graphically brought into everyone's living room where they result in a mixture of envy, resentment, admiration, self-satisfaction, guilt and indifference. Liberalization and globalization may have also undermined highly egalitarian domestic policies and the values associated with them. This is because of wider opportunities for successful entrepreneurs, stars, mobile firms and individuals and the highly educated Also, highly progressive tax structures are not easily enforceable, because rich people and capital are mobile and can avoid high rates.

However, it is difficult to seriously sustain the view that global economic integration is inexorably creating growing inequality. Those countries in southern Europe and East Asia which have most actively sought to develop through international economic integration have seen their income levels converge with those of the rich world. The largest concentration of global poverty is in India and China, both of which while now growing rapidly under the stimulus of economic reforms, opted to adhere to pursuer isolationist economic policies for several decades. The poorest countries, in Africa, have large numbers of subsistence farmers and have become marginalized from global economic integration because poor infrastructure and governance, as well as political instability, have prevented much meaningful development from taking place at all. The argument of anti-globalization critics that Africa has been impoverished by its cash-crop farming or multinational companies is a travesty of the truth. The former has, in fact, made a modest contribution to rural incomes and generally improved farming practices, and most of the latter have reduced their exposure to Africa.

Section 3 The international trade regime

(1) **Postwar Trade Regime**

The post-World War II trading system was born in conflict between American and British negotiators at the Bretton Woods Conference (1994). Reflecting their industrial supremacy, US negotiators wanted free trade and open foreign markets as soon as possible. Although the British were also committed to the principle of free trade, they were extremely concerned over the "dollar shortage," possible loss of domestic economic autonomy to pursue a full employment policy, and a number of related issues. The eventual compromise agreement to create the International Trade Organization (ITO) left many issues unresolved.

In 1948, the United States and its principal economic partners created the General Agreement on Tariffs and Trade (GATT) to promote "free and fairer" trade primarily through negotiated reductions of formal tariffs. When the ITO was turned down by the U.S. Senate in 1950, the GATT became the world's principal trade organization. The GATT is a fixed-rule trading system, and such a rule-based system is quite different from managed or "result-oriented" trade that sets quantitative targets or outcomes. The GATT was also based on the principle of multilateralism; trade rules were extended without discrimination to all members of the GATT. Unilateralism, bilateralism, and trading blocks were prohibited except in unusual cases. Another feature of the system was the principle of overall or general reciprocity; that is, trade liberalization and rules were to be determined by mutual balanced concessions. A system of specific reciprocity, on the other hand, requires that quite specific rather than general concessions must be traded. The GATT also incorporated provisions for the impartial adjudication of disputes.[5] Although the principles of the GATT trade regime were significantly qualified by escape clauses and exceptions, its creation was a major accomplishment as it has facilitated extremely important reductions of trade barriers.

The GATT proved remarkably successful in fostering trade liberalization and providing a framework for trade discussions. However, in contrast to the abandoned ITO, its authority and the scope of its responsibilities were severely limited. It was an essentially a negotiating forum rather than a true international organization and it had no rule-making authority. Moreover, it lacked an adequate dispute settlement mechanism, and its jurisdiction applied primarily to manufactured goods. The GATT had neither the authority to deal with agriculture, services, intellectual property rights, or foreign direct investment; nor did it have sufficient authority to deal with customer unions, and other preferential trading agreements. Its power to resolve trade disputes was also highly circumscribed. Successive American administrations and other governments became increasingly cognizant of the GATT's inherent limitations. Following the Uruguay Round, they incorporated it with the World Trade Organization (WTO) in 1995. As a full-fledged international organization rather than merely an international secretariat (like the GATT), the WTO's authority and responsibilities are much broder.

The GATT, and latter, the WTO, served the important political purpose of facilitating the reduction of trade barriers. The principle of comparative advantage indicates that a nation would increase its gains by opening its markets to foreign goods; also, an open economy would enjoy lower prices, consumer choice, and greater national efficiency. Nevertheless, because political losers would strongly oppose lifting trade barriers, proponents of free trade have to confront a mercantilist attitude that believes exports are good and imports are bad. This attitude is revealed when trade agreements are characterized as "concessions" to a foreign government. Because of this prevalent attitude, and for other political reasons, negotiated reductions of trade barriers based on the principle of reciprocity are necessary. The political logic of the GATT/WTO is that because liberalization harms certain interests that will inevitably oppose trade liberalization, it is necessary to liberalize in a coordinated way with concession for concession, thus making it easier to defeat protectionists. Once trade barriers have been lowered, a framework of agreements makes it quite difficult to raise them again.

The GATT, despite the limitations of its mandate and its cumbersome organizational structure, was important for many years in reducing barriers to international trade and in helping to establish rules to reduce trade conflict. The GATT provided a rule-based regime of trade liberalization founded on the principles of nondiscrimination, unconditional reciprocity, and transparency (for example, use of formal tariffs and publication of trade regulations). As trade relations constitute a Prisoner's Dilemma situation, unambiguous rules are required to forestall conflict.[6] Trade rules were determined and trade barriers were reduced through multilateral negotiations among GATT members. In effect, GATT members agreed to establish regulations lowering trade barriers and then let markets determine trade patterns; member states pledged not to resort to managed or results-oriented trade that set import quotas for particular products. Under GATT, markets were opened and new rules established by international negotiations; agreements were based on compromise or unconditional reciprocity rather than on unilateral actions by the strong or by specific reciprocity. GATT's goal was an open multilateralism; that is, the agreement provided for extension of negotiated trade rules to all members of the GATT without discrimination. However, candidates for membership did have to meet certain criteria and agree to obey its rules. The founders of the GATT wanted a steady progression toward an open world economy, with no return to the cycle of retaliation and counter retaliation that had characterized the 1930s.

The postwar period witnessed a number of agreements to lower tariff barriers. A significant shift in negotiations took place during the Kennedy Round (1964-1967). That Round, initiated by the United States as a response to growing concern over the possible trade diversion or discrimination consequences of the European Economic Community, substituted general reciprocity for the prior product-by-product approach to tariff cuts (specific reciprocity). GATT members agreed to reduce tariffs on particular products by certain percentages and make trade-offs across economic sectors. The Round resulted in a reduction of trade barriers on manufactures of approximately 33 percent and in a number of basic reforms, including regulation of "dumping" practices. In addition, preferential treatment was given to exports from less developed countries (LDCs).

The next major initiative to liberalize trade was the Tokyo Round (1973-1979), which after years of bitter fighting, proved far more comprehensive than earlier efforts. It included significant tariff cuts on most industrial products, liberalization of agricultural trade, and reduction of non-tariff barriers. In addition, the industrial countries pledged to pay greater attention to LDC demands for special treatment of their exports. However, the most important task of the Tokyo Round was to fashion codes of conduct to deal with unfair trade practices. To this end, the negotiations prohibited export subsidies and eliminated some discrimination in public procurement. However, that Round did not resolve the serious American-European dispute over agriculture, satisfy the LDCs, or stop the noxious proliferation of non-tariff barriers that occurred as a consequence of the New Protectionism that had commenced in the 1970s.[7]

Nevertheless, trade-liberalizing agreements did enable international trade to grow rapidly. Substantial expansion of trade meant that imports penetrated more deeply and trade became a much more important component in domestic economies. In fact, in some European Economic Community countries, exports soared. And even the domestic markets of the United States and Japan were internationalized to a significant extent. It is a particularly noteworthy that Japanese imports soon included a growing percentage of manufactured goods. Meanwhile, GATT membership greatly expanded over the years, and growing trade flows created a highly interdependent international economy, despite the 1970s slowdown.

(2) The Uruguay Round and World Trade Organization

By the mid-1980s, the Bretton Woods trade regime was no longer adequate to deal with a highly integrated world economy characterized by oligopolistic competition, scale economies, and dynamic comparative advantage. In addition, the New Protectionism of the 1970s had led to the erection of numerous non-tariff barriers, such as quotas and government subsidies.[8] Moreover, the character of trade itself was changing and outgrowing the rules and trading regime of the early postwar era. Trade became closely intertwined with the global activities of multinational firms, and trade in both services and manufactures expanded rapidly. Trade among industrialized countries became the most prominent feature of the trading system. In the 1980s the "new regionalism," especially acceleration of the movement toward European integration, was recognized as a threat to the multilateral trading system. From the early 1980s on the United States pressured its West European and other trading partners for a new round of trade negotiations to strengthen the multilateral trading system. Eventually, this American pressure overcame European and other resistance, and in 1986 the Uruguay Round of trade negotiations was launched at Punta del Este, Uruguay, resulting in intense negotiations until its conclusion in 1993.

The treaty produced by the Uruguay Round, which come into force on January 1, 1995, reduced tariffs on manufactured goods and lowered trade barriers in a number of important areas. At the same time that formal tariffs on merchandise goods were reduced to a very low level, the Uruguay Round decreased or eliminated many import quotas and subsidies. The agreement's twenty-nine separate accords also reduced trade barriers, and for the first time extended trade rules to a number of areas that included agriculture, textiles, services, intellectual property rights, and foreign investment. By one estimate, by the year 2002 the agreement should have increased world welfare by approximately $270 billion. While many economists and public officials praised the agreement, others emphasized the modesty of its gains. However, the long-term effects of these achievements remain in doubt. Speaking of the agreement, John Jackson, a leading expert on trade law, stated that the "devil is in the details."[9]

The Uruguay Round's most significant accomplishment was the creation of the World Trade Organization (WTO). In doing this, the Round took an important step toward completion of the framework of international institutions that had originally been proposed at Bretton Woods (1944). Although the WTO incorporated the GATT along with many of its rules and practices, the legal mandate and institutional structure of the WTO were designed to enable it to play a much more important role than the GATT had played in governance of international commerce. The WTO has more extensive and more binding rules. Moreover, the WTO has, in effect, the primary responsibility to facilitate international economic cooperation in trade liberalization and to fill in the many details omitted in the 22,000-page Uruguay Treaty. The agreement which established the WTO expanded and entrenched the GATT principal that trade should be governed by multilateral rules rather than by unilateral actions or bilateral negotiations.

The World Trade Organization (WTO) is, in essence, an American creation. The WTO's predecessor, the General Agreement on Tariffs and Trade (GATT) had well served American's fading mass-production economy, but it did not serve the emerging economy equally well. As a consequence of economic and technological developments prior to the Reagan Administration, the United States had become an increasingly service-oriented and high-tech economy. Therefore, in a major effort to reduce trade barriers, the Uruguay Round was initiated by the Reagan Administration and later was supported by the Bush Administration and, after much vacillation, by the Clinton Administration as well.

Although the WTO was not given as extensive rule-making authority as some desired, it does have much more authority than the GATT. The GATT dispute-settlement mechanism was incorporated in the WTO, reformed, and greatly strengthened by elimination of such basic flaws as long delays in the proceedings of dispute panels, the ability of disputants to block proceedings, and the frequent failure of members to implement decisions. The agreement also established a new appellate body to oversee the work of the dispute panels. Most importantly—and controversially—the WTO was empowered to levy fines on countries that refused to accept a decision of the dispute panel.

The institutional structure of the trade regime also changed significantly. Whereas the GATT had been a trade accord supported by a secretariat, the WTO is a membership organization that increases the legal coherence among its wide-ranging rights and obligations and establishes a permanent forum for negotiations. Biennial ministerial meetings should increase political guidance to the institution. The Uruguay Round also created a trade-policy-review mechanism to monitor member countries. With over 130 members, however, the WTO's ability to carry out its assigned responsibilities is subject to doubt.

Despite the impressive achievements of the Uruguay Round in reducing trade barriers, many vexing issues were left unresolved. Trade in certain areas such as agriculture, textiles, and shipping continues to be highly protected. The failure to reduce tariffs on agriculture and textiles was and continues to be especially vexing because lower tariffs would greatly benefit LDCs. Trade barriers are still high in most developing countries, especially with respect to services, and developed countries continue to restrict imports of automobiles, steel, textiles, consumer electronics, and agricultural products. Completion of the Uruguay Round's so-called "built-in" agenda is crucial, and the many issues unresolved at the close of the negotiations remain problematic. In addition, since the end of the Uruguay Round, a number of new and extremely difficult issues have surfaced, including labor standards, the environment, and human rights. Even more ominous, American public opinion has become more skeptical of the costs and benefits of trade, and by the late 1990s the WTO and trade liberalization were clearly on the defensive.

(1) Gray Burtless, Robert Z. Lawrence, Robert E. Litan, and Robert J. Shapiro, *Globaphobia: Confronting Fears about Open Trade* (Washington, D.C.: Brookings Institution, 1998), p.5-6

(2) Andrew Kohut, "Globalization and the Wage Gap," *New York Times*, 3 December 1999, sec. 1, reporting on a Pew Research Center's national survey in April 1999, which found that 52 percent of all respondents were negative toward globalization. Low-income families were much more negative than wealthier ones.

(3) First clearly described by Adam Smith.

(4) Maddison, A. *Monitoring the World Economy 1820-1992*, (Paris: Development Centre Studies, OECD, 1995)

(5) Jagdish Bhagwati, *The World Trading System at Risk* (Princeton: Princeton University Press, 1991).

(6) Avinash K. Dixit, *The Making of Economic Policy: A Transaction-Cost Politics Perspective* (Cambridge: MIT Press, 1996), p. 124.

(7) European Union agricultural subsidies are approximately $324 per acre in contrast to $34 per acre in the United States. *Burlington Free Press*, 12 December 1999, 3A.

(8) The New Protectionism, as distinct from the "old" protectionism, was characterized by hidden trade barriers, a shift from rules to discretion, and a return to liberalism. See W. M. Corden, *The Revival of Protectionism* (New York: Group of Thirty, 1984).

(9) The sheer magnitude of the agreement is extraordinary. As John Jackson has commented, the Uruguay Round negotiations were undoubtedly the most extensive ever carried out by any international organization. The agreement contained 22,000 pages and weighed 385 pounds. Although the agreement did not achieve many of the objectives sought by the United States, which had proposed the negotiations, it was an impressive achievement nevertheless. See John H. Jackson, in Peter B. Kenen, ed., *Managing the World Economy: Fifty Years After Bretton Woods* (Washington, D. C.: Institute for International Economics, 1994), p. 132f.

Chapter 4 The rise of Asian regionalism

Section 1 The experience of Asian financial crisis

In the summer of 1997, East Asian economies suffered a devastating blow. Economies that only four years earlier had been hailed by the World Bank as exemplars of "pragmatic orthodoxy" and as "remarkably successful in creating and sustaining macroeconomic stability" experienced the worst economic collapse of any countries since the 1930s and were declared victims of their own irresponsible ways. Beginning in Thailand in early July, the crisis spread rapidly up the East Asian coast and engulfed every nation in Southeast and East Asia. It had previously been unthinkable, given modern economic knowledge, that a financial crisis of this magnitude could occur. In fact, no one had predicted the crisis. In retrospect, however, a crisis of some sort appears to have been inevitable, given all the things that could and did go wrong in the months preceding it. In the language of social science, the East Asian financial crisis was over- determined. If one cause had not plunged the East Asian economies into crisis, there were half a dozen others that might have done so.

The East Asian economic crisis made more credible to many people the charge that economic globalization has significantly increased international economic instability and has been harmful to domestic societies. It is certainly undeniable that the economic plight of East Asia attests to the ability of international financial markets to wreak havoc on domestic economies. However, imprudent domestic economic policies were as important as global economic forces in making these economies highly vulnerable to sudden shifts in international financial flows. Many of the allegedly negative effects of economic globalization are actually due either to poor economic management by governments or to developments that have nothing whatsoever to do with economic globalization. The victims in these situations have generally been small economies. The United States has run a trade/payments deficit for approximately three decades without unleashing any dire consequences. While large states with large markets and resources may be able to defy economic forces for a long time, such a privilege is rarely accorded to small states, especially small states with such reckless policies as borrowing "short" and lending "long"; that is, those who finance long-term development and risky projects with short maturity funds.

It is extraordinary that there is no mechanism to regulate international finance. Even though the world economy experienced three major financial crisis in the 1990s—the 1992-

1993 crisis of the ERM, the 1994-1995 Mexican/Latin American crisis, and, beginning in 1997, the East Asian crisis—efforts to create effective regulations governing international capital flows and financial matters have not made much progress. A number of scholars, including Paul Kindleberger, Susan Strange, and James Tobin note that the international financial system is the weakest link in the chain of the international economy and that international finance should be regulated effectively. Financial markets, these scholars have argued, are too subject to irrational manias and crises and cannot police themselves. In such a situation, it is quite unfair to blame the East Asian crisis solely on the forces of economic globalization and on "wicked" Western speculators like George Soros.

Although destabilized financial markets will eventually return to an equilibrium, the crisis can impose an unacceptably heavy cost on innocent bystanders and on the larger world economy. For this reason, scholars such as Kindleberger, Strange and Tobin advocated establishment of international regulations or formal regime to govern financial markets. For example, Tobin and others have proposed an international tax to discourage financial speculation, especially in short-term investments. Others, such as George Soros, go father and argue that creation of an international central bank and true "lender of last resort" should be at the heart of a mechanism to govern international finance; that is, an authority should be created to function internationally as central banks do domestically. Then, when a government finds itself in trouble, the international bank could step in to rescue it. It is not necessary to say that the prospects of establishing such an international central bank are quite remote, at least under the political conditions of the early twenty-first century.

In the late summer of 1998, the East Asian economic crisis spilled over into the global economy, setting the stage for what President Clinton declared the worst economic crisis in fifty years. The Russian government's devaluation of the ruble against the German mark by about 40 percent in late August triggered the globalization of the crisis. The Clinton Administration, for political reasons, had bet heavily on "saving" Russia and had pressured the IMF to loan Russia tens of billions of dollars, many of which were subsequently squandered and funneled to private Russian accounts in foreign banks. Investors and governments around the world panicked as they witnessed a major nuclear power reneging on its agreements and facing economic/political chaos. Worried that other countries would also default, investors searching for safe havens in the early fall of 1998 began to withdraw funds from LDCs. Declining corporate profits and investor panic led to a precipitous fall of the American and other stock markets (October 31, 1998). The threat that the Long-Term Management Fund would collapse greatly deepened the crisis. These events in turn set off a serious credit crunch that further slowed global economic growth. Late that fall, some estimated that approximately one-third of the world economy was in recession; the United States alone was still experiencing economic growth. With the depression in East Asia and recession in much of the rest of the world, commodity prices fell considerably, and this caused economic distress in many commodity-exporting sectors, including American agriculture.

American officials had become concerned in the early fall that the financial crisis would continue to spread and had focused much of their attention on Brazil. Brazil possessed many of the characteristics of a developing economy in serious trouble, including a huge budget deficit and sizable international dept. The country's uncertain fiscal situation was accompanied by a heavy capital outflow and put severe pressure on the Brazilian real. The Clinton Administration feared that financial collapse in Brazil, a major importer of American products, would seriously damage the American economy and accelerate turmoil throughout the world. As the troubles of the global economy continued to unfold, the Clinton Administration took action. In a well-publicized speech in mid-September to the New York Council on Foreign Relations, the President proposed that all the major economic powers stimulate their own economies in order to restore global economic growth; he also proposed that the major economic powers should meet at the time of the next IMF/World Bank meeting in October to develop a longer-term solution to the problem of global financial instability.

These Clinton initiatives were given a cool reception. Every central bank ignored the suggestion that interest rates be cut in order to stimulate global growth. Nevertheless, on October 15, the Federal Reserve, motivated primarily by concerns about the American economy, did cut interest rates; it did so twice more before the end of November. These important moves restored investor confidence and succeeded in reinvigorating the American economy. The other major economic powers had agreed, although without enthusiasm, to Clinton's proposal that they meet. That meeting took place during the annual joint meeting of the IMF and World Bank (WB) which was held in Washington in late October.

At the IMF-WB meetings, President Clinton set forth proposals for a "new international financial architecture" to contain the spreading economic crisis and prevent future crisis. The Administration also hoped to forestall efforts by other governments (mainly Western Europe and Japan) to impose new restrictions on international capital flows. The President's proposals were considered at the October 30 meeting of the major economic powers, and several important decisions were reached. The G-7, assuming that investors would not repeat the mistakes made in Mexico (1994-1995) and East Asia if they were fully aware of risky situations, agreed that much greater transparency of financial conditions in every country was crucial to the prevention of future financial crisis. In addition, the G-7 called for much tighter international standards for accounting and for bank regulation.

The most important G-7 decision was to accept Clinton's proposal that the IMF should establish a $90 billion contingency fund to provide countries with emergency financial assistance; the fund would help only those countries already carrying out economic reforms and those whose economic "fundamentals" were basically sound. Before a crisis actually occurred, this would enable the IMF to intervene in order to shore up the country's financial defenses of its currency by providing adequate liquidity and thereby preventing financial panic. When it made this proposal, the Clinton Administration had Brazil in mind, as Brazil required a huge infusion of foreign capital to keep its economy afloat. Following a bruising but ultimately successful battle in the Congress over replenishment of IMF funds, much of which had previously been squandered in Russia, the IMF offered Brazil a large assistance package of over $40 billion in November. A precondition that the Brazilian economy be significantly overhauled was attached. In early 1999, having failed to improve its economic performance, Brazil suffered a major economic crisis.

As important as the G-7 decisions had been, they failed to quell the intense controversy over reform and regulation of the international financial system. By early 2000, a number of proposals had been formulated to deal with destabilizing international financial flows. Current proposals range from creation of a worldwide central bank to imposition of an international tax on financial transfers across national boundaries (called the "Tobin Tax"[1]). Some experts believe that self-imposed national restrictions on both financial inflows and outflows are necessary. A number of governments such as Japan, China, Malaysia, and Chile have, in fact, instituted controls on financial flows. The European Union, too, has begun consideration of some regional regulations on capital flows. This experience of financial crisis made Asian countries promote Asian financial and economic cooperation (details are mentioned in chapter 8).

Section 2   The promotion of regional trade

(1) Bilateral trade agreement

The data on trade flows are from the IMF's *Direction of Trade Statistics*.

In the Asia-Pacific, the financial crisis continues to be a watershed. Since that crisis, the strategies for shaping external economic relations have changed, both in trade and in finance. Before 1997, the emphasis was on multilateral organizations, i.e. on the International Monetary Fund and on the World Trade Organization. Today, two trends are emerging—monetary regionalism in finance and bilateralism in trade. The change is less visible in finance, where progress to date is somewhat limited. By contrast, bilateral trade agreements are truly mushrooming in East Asia. For instance, China has already sealed or is currently negotiating free trade agreements with 25 countries—up from zero two years ago.[2]

Conventional regional integration, i.e. free trade areas and customs unions with more than two participating countries, is in decline in the region. APEC in particular is no longer exhibiting the dynamics of the early 1990s. APEC is too large to effective, and it suffers from American dominance. By contrast, both bilateral trade agreements and the emerging monetary cooperation scheme in the Asia-Pacific are implemented without U.S. participation. Notable exceptions are the Australian-American and Singapore-U.S. free trade agreement.

The current bilateral wave and other preferential trade agreements are having severe repercussions for the WTO. In 2005, for the first time ever, more trade occurred under the preferential agreements than under the most-favored-nation clause, article one of the General Agreement on Tariffs and Trade.[3] The most-favored-nation clause has degenerated into the least-favored-nation clause, as the American trade economist Jagdish Bhagwati has been proclaiming. The European Union was the original culprit. Although the EU has not been implementing new free trade agreements in recent years, due to a number of initiatives, some of them overlapping, the EU has contributed to the undermining of the multilateral regime. As a result of the generalized system of preferences, the everything but arms initiative, and free trade agreements, the EU trades with just eight—out of 148 WTO member countries—under the most-favored-nation clause. These are the United States, Canada, Australia, Japan, New Zealand, Hong Kong, Singapore and South Korea.[4]

Today, there are more than 300 free trade agreements and a few customs unions either already implemented or being negotiated. Until a few years ago, the entire Asia-Pacific region was not contributing to this trend. Countries like Japan and South Korea were staunch supporters of the multilateral regime. This however, has changed dramatically. Partly because there continues to be a momentum for bilateral agreements and partly because some countries in the region are using these agreements to fast-forward their economic and political position in the region, no country in the Asia-Pacific is willing to abstain from the current trend.

The traditional debate on this issue has been characterized by the stepping-stone or stumbling bloc argument. Bilateral or multilateral agreements could be either contributing to improvements of the multilateral regime or undermining it. Until today, it appears fair to say that the multilateral regime has received very little, if any, stimulus from bilateral agreements. They exist parallel to the WTO, and there are features of bilateral agreements which suggest that they undermine the multilateral order. For instance, many bilateral deals contain dispute settlement mechanisms outside the WTO. This feature of bilateral agreements is not necessary, because dispute settlement could continue to be conducted in Geneva. The fact that this is not the case, in particular in agreements in which the USA participates, indicates that bilateral agreements are competing and not complementing the multilateral regime.

(2) Bilateral trade agreements as positional goods

One aspect of bilateral trade agreements that has been somewhat overseen is the possibility that bilaterals are positional goods. Fred Hirsch has defined it as such: "Positional goods are losing their utility if others are using the same good." For instance, using a motor car has a higher utility when very few others are doing the same thing. If everybody drives a car, the utility of having a car declines sharply.

Bilateral trade agreements could also be positional goods. If all others countries rely on market access via the multilateral regime, then a bilateral free trade agreement could be beneficial, provided that market access is unrestricted in the bilateral agreement and is more restricted under WTO regulations. For instance, if Singapore were the only country that has successfully negotiated a free trade agreement with the United States, Singapore would have a benefit. If all other WTO member countries would also negotiate a similar free trade agreement with the U.S., there would not be any additional advantage from a bilateral trade agreement, whilst the disadvantages of free trade agreements would continue to exist. Simply stated, the more countries use bilateral agreements, the more limited is their utility. There continue to be advantages for early starters, but as other countries catchup, the usefulness of bilateral agreements declines. Assuming a scenario in which all WTO member countries would have implemented a free trade agreement with the U.S. the utility of such an agreement—compared with the multilateral alternative—would not be large. Only if the United States would have a protectionist trade regime under WTO regulations and a significantly more open bilateral regime, there would be some continuing advantage.

However, a brief look at existing bilateral or regional agreements would induce the assumption that such a scenario is unlikely. For instance, there have been continuing quarrels between the US and Canada over the implementation of the NAFTA free trade agreement. Canada has frequently accused the US of protectionist policies in some sectors, most prominently in softwood lumber, but Canada was unable to secure free trade within NAFTA in specific areas.

The Canadian-American clash on softwood lumber highlights the importance of dispute settlement. Prior to the creation of the WTO in 1995, dispute settlement could be blacked by the party accused of an illegitimate policy. This has changed. Today, the WTO is one of the few multilateral organizations where small countries can take the EU or the USA to court and have a fair chance of receiving justice, if after some years. No party can bloc the dispute settlement mechanism of the WTO. The implementation of the dispute settlement mechanism in the WTO was not only a milestone for the creation of a rules-based system of international trade, but can at the same time be interpreted as one of the few building blocs for global governance. If anything, an expansion of the WTO's mandate can be considered a useful step.

By contrast, transferring dispute settlement to the bilateral level is a deterioration. In many bilateral schemes, there is an option—either bilateral dispute settlement or multilateral dispute settlement. It is obvious that the bilateral route offers many possibilities for the more powerful partners to promote their case. Hierarchy and power—never fully absent in international trade—have a more prominent role in bilateral trade agreements than in the multilateral regime. The existence of an alternative to the WTO dispute settlement mechanism provides the more powerful countries with an additional choice, but for weaker countries this is a drawback.

Another disadvantage of free trade agreements that will not disappear over time is the administrative burden that rules of origin cause. Even if there is no significant utility of bilateral free trade agreements because of widespread implementation of these treaties, these disadvantages will remain.

Section 3 Chinese economic development

(1) China and other Asian countries

Over the past 25 years or so, China's economic performance has been spectacular, averaging real GDP growth of 9.6% a year, and external trade growth of 14.6%. China recently released a growth figure of 9.9% for 2005 after having revised GDP figures substantially for the period 1993-2004. This growth rate for 2005 leaves little doubt that China has been, and will continue to be, a major driver of growth in Asia.

China's efforts to open up to the outside world have been extremely positive - not only for the country itself, but for the region as a whole. Spurred by strong processing exports and domestic demand, China's imports from Asia have soared. China has now overtaken the US as the single largest export market for Korea, absorbing 24.5% of its exports in 2004. China is also an important and growing market for Japan, Malaysia, Philippines, Singapore and Thailand, and a key driver of regional integration.

Obviously, with its sheer size and rapid climb up the value-added chain, China's emergence as a manufacturing base has greatly modified the global competition landscape. In the short run, economies that are slow to adapt to the changing dynamics of comparative advantage could face more direct competition. However, for most Asian economies, the new growth dividend of China's expansion can also facilitate adjustment to a more integrated regional economy. Over the medium to long-term, China's economy offers tremendous opportunities for Asian exporters of primary commodities, manufacturing inputs and final goods, which will more than compensate for the challenges it has brought.

(2) The Challenges Ahead

The benefits for China itself are clear and measurable. Sustained, rapid, economic growth and targeted government programs have put China ahead of schedule in achieving many of the Millennium Development Goals (MDGs). For example, the proportion of the population living on less than $1 per day has already fallen from 33% in 1990 to 10.4% in 2004 - well ahead of the MDG target for cutting absolute poverty rates by half by 2015.

Having come this far, China is well positioned to take the next steps on its journey to sustainable growth and prosperity - steps to make growth more inclusive and further reduce poverty, to improve governance and promote stronger social development, and to counter the negative environmental impacts of growth.

Despite notable progress in poverty reduction, China still has a very large population of poor people. Again using the $1 per day guideline, about 135 million people were classified as poor in 2004 against the international standard. The speed of poverty reduction has slowed, partly due to slow growth in rural income in recent years. Moreover, income distribution actually worsened in the past two decades.

If economic growth is to benefit most of the population - especially the poor - it must be equitable and inclusive. While some deterioration in income distribution is inevitable as China moves from a centrally planned to a market economy, the speed of the growing inequality is worrying. China's income inequality is now above the average of many regions.

Poor interior regions have not benefited as much from economic growth and reforms as the east coast. Per capita GDP in the interior is less than half that along the east coast. The Asian Development Bank (ADB) business climate survey found that about 39% of foreign companies operating in China would not consider expanding their operations into the interior provinces, mainly because of a lack of markets and poor infrastructure.

In addition to income inequalities, education, health, social security and gender disparities have widened among some segments of society. Compared to other developing economies, China has shown impressive progress toward eliminating illiteracy and achieving universal, 9-year compulsory education. But disparities persist in education access, quality, and outcomes across regional, urban-rural, and gender dimensions.

Similarly, there is still a large gap in the quality of health services between rural and urban areas. Health insurance systems largely exclude rural residents and migrant workers. Overemphasis on the "user pays" principle in compulsory education and public health threatens social service access for poor households.

About the solution of these problems, what shall they do?

With about 60% of the population engaged in the agriculture sector, improving the performance of agriculture is the direct way to reduce urban-rural inequalities. Given the arable land and water constraints, agricultural development needs to focus on improving rural infrastructure, diversifying crop production, and adopting integrated, environmentally friendly approaches to farming. Rebuilding the rural financial system would also relieve the lack of financial services that constrains farmers' investment options.

Creating sufficient job opportunities for the 150 million surplus rural laborers is also critically important. This is a major and ongoing challenge which will require greater SME and private sector development, as well as vocational training for rural migrants. Furthermore, if China is to avoid the urban poverty and slums that are evident in many of the world's mega cities, the Government has to learn from the lessons of urban development in Asian and Latin American countries - lessons like the importance of urban housing, infrastructure and social safety nets.

In the short term, however, priority should be given to the poorest of the poor and poorest rural areas. A recent ADB study shows that a basic social development and poverty reduction program for rural areas would be affordable even in the current fiscal circumstances. For a cost of additional RMB100 billion a year, with in two to three years, the Government could

   a. establish a rural minimum living standard support system to help about 25 million of the poorest people,
   b. provide free 9 year compulsory education for 120 million students in rural areas;
   c. establish a basic rural health care system to cover all 770 million farmers; and
   d. speed up the participative poverty reduction program in the 148,000 poorest villages nationwide.

It seems to be ambitious, but it's achievable. Given that fiscal revenue increased by about RMB 500 billion per year in the past two years, such an outlay is quite feasible, and would go a long way to making growth more inclusive and equitable.

(3) **Governance for Social and Economic Development**

Beyond its economic and social dimensions, China's transition from a centrally planned to a market economy marks a fundamental change in the system of governance. In our view, continued reform in the legal and regulatory system is needed to support the market economy and to conform to WTO rules. In order to minimize waste of public resources and reduce corruption, considerable work needs to be done to improve the country's auditing and accounting system. It is also important to build local public administration capabilities in the central and western provinces and support efforts to broaden public participation, particularly by the poor, in decisions that affect them. In all of these areas, ADB could continue to provide assistance and bring global best practices to China.

Our experience has taught us that sustainable social and economic development requires strong government partnerships with civil society. The 1990s witnessed an explosive growth of NGOs in almost all Asian countries. I am pleased to note that the Government of China has taken steps to increase public participation, with a positive role for NGOs. Recently, for example, ADB assisted Jianxi province involve NGOs at the village level in implementation of a poverty reduction project. This is the first time China has allowed NGOs to participate in social services using large scale public resources.

(4) Environmental Sustainability and Energy Conservation

Turning to the environment, it is clear that here; too, China faces a very large challenge. Inappropriate pricing, use of obsolete, polluting technologies, limited natural resources and weaknesses in environmental management have left a legacy of land degradation, poor and declining water quality, air pollution and acid rain. Over the next two to three decades, rapid growth, industrialization and urbanization will place even greater pressure on China's environment and natural resources.

ADB is actively assisting China to deal with these issues. By the end of 2005, ADB had provided over $3.4 billion in loans to support environmental improvement. In their view, increasing investment in the environment from both public and private sources, and more closely involving private companies, NGOs and the general public in environmental protection, should be top priorities as China continues to grow.

Improving the transparency of environmental legal and regulatory processes, along with stronger enforcement, are important elements of environmental sustainability. While good progress has been made in water tariff reform, there is a need to strengthen wastewater tariff and solid waste charges reforms. Pricing policies, too, should encourage use of cleaner energies and reduce air pollution.

Due consideration must be given to sustaining energy resources in China. The demand for energy continues to outpace supply, resulting in shortages of petroleum products and electricity. The large share of manufacturing in China has led to concerns regarding the country's relatively high energy intensity. The projected GDP growth rate of over 7% to 2020, along with rapid urbanization and motorization will add to the stress.

Energy conservation can only be achieved through a comprehensive approach that includes energy system optimization, construction of cogeneration power plants and energy efficient buildings, demand side management and capacity building for promoting and implementing energy conservation projects. I am pleased to know that the Government recognizes the enormous potential for, and the benefits of, energy conservation. In its recently approved 11th Five Year Program, the Government targets a decrease in energy consumption per unit of GDP output by 20% by 2010.

(1) An excellent discussion of international financial reform is Barry J. Eichengreen, *Towards a New International Financial Architecture: A Practical Post-Asian Agenda* (Washington, D.C.: Institute for International Economics, 1999).
(2) The Wall Street Journal, (3 October 2005:1)
(3) Although the GATT Secretariat does no longer exist and has been replaced by the WTO, the GATT treaty—in its 1994 version— continues to be the legal basis of the multilateral trading regime. The General Agreement on Trade in Services (GATS) regulates services, including financial services.
(4) The World Trade Organization, (2004: 21)

Chapter 5 The three theoretical facets of Asian regionalism

Section 1 Global environmental crisis

(1) Growing population

Population, as Malthus said, naturally tends to grow "geometrically," or, as we would now say, exponentially. In a finite world this means that the per capita share of the world's goods must steadily decrease. Is ours a finite world?

A fair defense can be put forward for the view that the world is infinite; or that we do not know that it is not. But, in terms of the practical problems that we must face in the next few generations with the foreseeable technology, it is clear that we will greatly increase human misery if we do not, during the immediate future, assume that the world available to the terrestrial human population is finite. "Space" is no escape.[1] A finite world can support only a finite population; therefore, population growth must eventually equal zero. (The case of perpetual wide fluctuations above and below zero is a trivial variant that need not be discussed.) When this condition is met, what will be the situation of mankind? Specifically, can Bentham's goal of "the greatest good for the greatest number" be realized?

No--for two reasons, each sufficient by itself. The first is a theoretical one. It is not mathematically possible to maximize for two (or more) variables at the same time. This was clearly stated by von Neumann and Morgenstern,[2] but the principle is implicit in the theory of partial differential equations, dating back at least to D'Alembert (1717-1783). The second reason springs directly from biological facts. To live, any organism must have a source of energy (for example, food). This energy is utilized for two purposes: mere maintenance and work. For man, maintenance of life requires about 1600 kilocalories a day ("maintenance calories"). Anything that he does over and above merely staying alive will be defined as work, and is supported by "work calories" which he takes in. Work calories are used not only for what we call work in common speech; they are also required for all forms of enjoyment, from swimming and automobile racing to playing music and writing poetry. If our goal is to maximize population it is obvious what we must do: We must make the work calories per person approach as close to zero as possible. No gourmet meals, no vacations, no sports, no music, no literature, no art,... I think that everyone will grant, without argument or proof, that maximizing population does not maximize goods. Bentham's goal is impossible.

In reaching this conclusion I have made the usual assumption that it is the acquisition of energy that is the problem. The appearance of atomic energy has led some to question this assumption. However, given an infinite source of energy, population growth still produces an inescapable problem. The problem of the acquisition of energy is replaced by the problem of its dissipation, as J. H. Fremlin has so wittily shown.[3] The arithmetic signs in the analysis are, as it were, reversed; but Bentham's goal is still unobtainable.

The optimum population is, then, less than the maximum. The difficulty of defining the optimum is enormous; so far as I know, no one has seriously tackled this problem. Reaching an acceptable and stable solution will surely require more than one generation of hard analytical work--and much persuasion.

We want the maximum good per person; but what is good? To one person it is wilderness, to another it is ski lodges for thousands. To one it is estuaries to nourish ducks for hunters to shoot; to another it is factory land. Comparing one good with another is, we usually say, impossible because goods are incommensurable. Incommensurables cannot be compared.

Theoretically this may be true; but in real life incommensurables are commensurable. Only a criterion of judgment and a system of weighting are needed. In nature the criterion is survival. Is it better for a species to be small and hideable, or large and powerful? Natural selection commensurates the incommensurables. The compromise achieved depends on a natural weighting of the values of the variables.

Man must imitate this process. There is no doubt that in fact he already does, but unconsciously. It is when the hidden decisions are made explicit that the arguments begin. The problem for the years ahead is to work out an acceptable theory of weighting. Synergistic effects, nonlinear variation, and difficulties in discounting the future make the intellectual problem difficult, but not (in principle) insoluble.

Has any cultural group solved this practical problem at the present time, even on an intuitive level? One simple fact proves that none has: there is no prosperous population in the world today that has, and has had for some time, a growth rate of zero. Any people that has intuitively identified its optimum point will soon reach it, after which its growth rate becomes and remains zero.

Of course, a positive growth rate might be taken as evidence that a population is below its optimum. However, by any reasonable standards, the most rapidly growing populations on earth today are (in general) the most miserable. This association (which need not be invariable) casts doubt on the optimistic assumption that the positive growth rate of a population is evidence that it has yet to reach its optimum.

We can make little progress in working toward optimum population size until we explicitly exorcize the spirit of Adam Smith in the field of practical demography. In economic affairs, *The Wealth of Nations* (1776) popularized the "invisible hand," the idea that an individual who "intends only his own gain," is, as it were, "led by an invisible hand to promote... the public interest"[(4)]. Adam Smith did not assert that this was invariably true, and perhaps neither did any of his followers. But he contributed to a dominant tendency of thought that has ever since interfered with positive action based on rational analysis, namely, the tendency to assume that decisions reached individually will, in fact, be the best decisions for an entire society. If this assumption is correct it justifies the continuance of our present policy of laissez-faire in reproduction. If it is correct we can assume that men will control their individual fecundity so as to produce the optimum population. If the assumption is not correct, we need to reexamine our individual freedoms to see which ones are defensible.

(2) Tragedy of Freedom in a Commons

The rebuttal to the invisible hand in population control is to be found in a scenario first sketched in a little-known pamphlet[(5)] in 1833 by a mathematical amateur named William Forster Lloyd (1794-1852). We may well call it "the tragedy of the commons" using the word "tragedy" as the philosopher Whitehead used it[(6)]: "The essence of dramatic tragedy is not unhappiness. It resides in the solemnity of the remorseless working of things." He then goes on to say, "This inevitableness of destiny can only be illustrated in terms of human life by incidents which in fact involve unhappiness. For it is only by them that the futility of escape can be made evident in the drama."

The tragedy of the commons develops in this way, Picture a pasture open to all. It is to be expected that each herdsman will try to keep as many cattle as possible on the commons. Such an arrangement may work reasonably satisfactorily for centuries because tribal wars, poaching, and disease keep the numbers of both man and beast well below the carrying capacity of the land. Finally, however, comes the day of reckoning, that is, the day when the long-desired goal of social stability be comes a reality. At this point, the inherent logic of the commons remorselessly generates tragedy.

As a rational being, each herdsman seeks to maximize his gain. Explicitly or implicitly, more or less consciously, he asks, "What is the utility to me of adding one more animal to my herd?" This utility has one negative and one positive component.

> a. The positive component is a function of the increment of one animal. Since the herdsman receives all the proceeds from the sale of the additional animal, the positive utility is nearly +1.
> b. The negative component is a function of the additional overgrazing created by one more animal. Since, however, the effects of overgrazing are shared by all the herdsmen, the negative utility for any particular decision-making herdsman is only a fraction of −1.

Adding together the component partial utilities, the rational herdsman concludes that the only sensible course for him to pursue is to add another animal to his herd. And another; and another.... But this is the conclusion reached by each and every rational herdsman sharing a commons. Therein is the tragedy. Each man is locked into a system that compels him to increase his herd without limit - in a world that is limited. Ruin is the destination toward which all men rush, each pursuing his own best interest in a society that believes in the freedom of the commons. Freedom in a commons brings ruin to all.

Some would say that this is a platitude. Would that it were! In a sense, it was learned thousands of years ago, but natural selection favors the forces of psychological denial.[7] The individual benefits as an individual from his ability to deny the truth even though society as a whole, of which he is a part, suffers.

Education can counteract the natural tendency to do the wrong thing, but the inexorable succession of generations requires that the basis for this knowledge be constantly refreshed.

A simple incident that occurred a few years ago in Leominster, Massachusetts, shows how perishable the knowledge is. During the Christmas shopping season the parking meters downtown were covered with red with plastic bags that bore tags reading: "Do not open until after Christmas. Free parking courtesy of the mayor and city council." In other words, facing the prospect of an increased demand for already scarce space, the city fathers reinstituted the system of the commons. (Cynically, we suspect that they gained more votes than they lost by this retrogressive act.)

In an approximate way, the logic of commons has been understood for a long time, perhaps since the discovery of agriculture or the invention of private property in real estate. But it is understood mostly only in special cases which are not sufficiently generalized. Even at this late date, cattlemen leasing national land on the western ranges demonstrate no more than an ambivalent understanding, in constantly pressuring federal authorities to increase head count to the point where overgrazing produces erosion and weed dominance. Likewise, the oceans of the world continue to suffer from the survival of the philosophy of the commons. Maritime nations still respond automatically to the shibboleth of the "freedom of the seas." Professing to believe in "inexhaustible resources of the oceans," they bring species after species of fish and whales closer to extinction.[8]

The National Parks present another instance of the working out of the tragedy of the commons. At present, are open to all, without limit. The parks themselves are limited in extent-there is only one Yosemite Valley--whereas population seems to grow without limit. The values that visitors seek the parks are steadily eroded. Plainly, we must soon cease to treat the parks as commons or they will be of no value anyone.

What shall we do? We have several options. We might sell them off as private property.

We might keep them as public property, but allocate the right enter them. The allocation might be on the basis of wealth, by the use of an auction system. It might be on the basis merit, as defined by some agreed upon standards. It might be by lottery. Or it might be on a first-come, first served basis, administered to long queues. These, I think, are all the reasonable possibilities. They are all objectionable. But we must choose---or acquiesce in the destruction of the commons that we call our National Parks.

(3) Pollution

In a reverse way, the tragedy of the commons reappears in problems of pollution. Here it is not a question of taking something out of the commons, but of putting something in-- sewage, or chemical, radioactive, and heat wastes into water; noxious and dangerous fumes into the air and distracting and unpleasant advertising signs into the line of sight. The calculations of utility are much the same as before. The rational man finds that his share of the cost of the wastes he discharges into the commons is less than the cost of purifying his wastes before releasing them. Since this is true for everyone, we are locked into a system of "fouling our own nest," so long as we behave only as independent, rational, free-enterprises.

The tragedy of the commons as a food basket is averted by private property, or something formally like it. But the air and waters surrounding us cannot readily be fenced, and so the tragedy of the commons as a cesspool must be prevented by different means, by coercive laws or taxing devices that make it cheaper for the polluter to treat his pollutants than to discharge them untreated. We have not progressed as far with the solution of this problem as we have with the first. Indeed, our particular concept of private property, which deters us from exhausting the positive resources of the earth, favors pollution. The owner of a factory on the bank of a stream--whose property extends to the middle of the stream often has difficulty seeing why it is not his natural right to muddy the waters flowing past his door. The law, always behind the times, requires elaborate stitching and fitting to adapt it to this newly perceived aspect of the commons. The pollution problem is a consequence of population. It did not much matter how a lonely American frontiersman disposed of his waste. As population became denser, the natural chemical and biological recycling processes became overloaded, calling for a redefinition of property rights.

(4) How to Legislate Temperance

Analysis of the pollution problem as a function of population density uncovers a not generally recognized principle of morality, namely: the morality of an act is a function of the state of the system at the time it is performed[9]. Using the commons as a cesspool does not harm the general public under frontier conditions, because there is no public; the same behavior in a metropolis is unbearable. A hundred and fifty years ago a plainsman could kill an American bison, cut out only the tongue for his dinner, and discard the rest of the animal. He was not in any important sense being wasteful. Today, with only a few thousand bison left, we would be appalled at such behavior.

In passing, it is worth noting that the morality of an act cannot be determined from a photograph. One does not know whether a man killing an elephant or setting fire to the grassland is harming others until one knows the total system in which his act appears. "One picture is worth a thousand words," said an ancient Chinese; but it may take 10,000 words to validate it. It is as tempting to ecologists as it is to reformers in general to try to persuade others by way of the photographic shortcut. But the essence of an argument cannot be photographed: it must be presented rationally --in words.

That morality is system-sensitive escaped the attention of most codifiers of ethics in the past. "Thou shalt not..." is the form of traditional ethical directives which make no allowance for particular circumstances. The laws of our society follow the pattern of ancient ethics, and therefore are poorly suited to governing a complex, crowded, changeable world. Our epicyclic solution is to augment statutory law with administrative law. Since it is practically impossible to spell out all the conditions under which it is safe to burn trash in the back yard or to run an automobile without smog-control, by law we delegate the details to bureaus. The result is administrative law, which is rightly feared for an ancient reason— *Quis custodiet ipsos custodes*? "Who shall watch the watchers themselves?" John Adams said that we must have a government of laws and not men." Bureau administrators, trying to evaluate the morality of acts in the total system, are singularly liable to corruption, producing a government by men, not laws.

Prohibition is easy to legislate (though not necessarily to enforce); but how do we legislate temperance? Experience indicates that it can be accomplished best through the mediation of administrative law. We limit possibilities unnecessarily if we suppose that the sentiment of *Quis custodiet* denies us the use of administrative law. We should rather retain the phrase as a perpetual reminder of fearful dangers we cannot avoid. The great challenge facing us now is to invent the corrective feedbacks that are needed to keep custodians honest. We must find ways to legitimate the needed authority of both the custodians and the corrective feedbacks.

(5) Freedom to Breed Is Intolerable

The tragedy of the commons is involved in population problems in another way. In a world governed solely by the principle of "dog eat dog"--if indeed there ever was such a world-how many children a family had would not be a matter of public concern. Parents who bred too exuberantly would leave fewer descendants, not more, because they would be unable to care adequately for their children. David Lack and others have found that such a negative feedback demonstrably controls the fecundity of birds.(10) But men are not birds, and have not acted like them for millenniums, at least.

If each human family were dependent only on its own resources; *if* the children of improvident parents starved to death; *if*, thus, over breeding brought its own "punishment" to the germ line-*then* there would be no public interest in controlling the breeding of families. But our society is deeply committed to the welfare state,(11) and hence is confronted with another aspect of the tragedy of the commons.

In a welfare state, how shall we deal with the family, the religion, the race, or the class (or indeed any distinguishable and cohesive group) that adopts over breeding as a policy to secure its own aggrandizement?(12) To couple the concept of freedom to breed with the belief that everyone born has an equal right to the commons is to lock the world into a tragic course of action.

Unfortunately this is just the course of action that is being pursued by the United Nations. In late 1967, some 30 nations agreed to the following:(13)

The Universal Declaration of Human Rights describes the family as the natural and fundamental unit of society. It follows that any choice and decision with regard to the size of the family must irrevocably rest with the family itself, and cannot be made by anyone else.

It is painful to have to deny categorically the validity of this right; denying it, one feels as uncomfortable as a resident of Salem, Massachusetts, who denied the reality of witches in the 17th century. At the present time, in liberal quarters, something like a taboo acts to inhibit criticism of the United Nations. There is a feeling that the United Nations is "our last and best hope," that we shouldn't find fault with it; we shouldn't play into the hands of the archconservatives. However, let us not forget what Robert Louis Stevenson said: "The truth that is suppressed by friends is the readiest weapon of the enemy." If we love the truth we must openly deny the validity of the Universal Declaration of Human Rights, even though it is promoted by the United Nations. We should also join with Kingsley Davis(14) in attempting to get planned Parenthood-World Population to see the error of its ways in embracing the same tragic ideal.

(6) Conscience is Self-Eliminating

It is a mistake to think that we can control the breeding of mankind in the long run by an appeal to conscience. Charles Galton Darwin made this point when he spoke on the centennial of the publication of his grandfather's great book. The argument is straightforward and Darwinian.

People vary. Confronted with appeals to limit breeding, some people will undoubtedly respond to the plea more than others. Those who have more children will produce a larger fraction of the next generation than those with more susceptible consciences. The difference will be accentuated, generation by generation.

In C. G. Darwin's words: "It may well be that it would take hundreds of generations for the progenitive instinct to develop in this way, but if it should do so, nature would have taken her revenge, and the variety *Homo contracipiens* would become extinct and would be replaced by the variety *Homo progenitivus*"[15].

The argument assumes that conscience or the desire for children (no matter which) is hereditary--but hereditary only in the most general formal sense. The result will be the same whether the attitude is transmitted through germ-cells, or exosomatically, to use A. J. Lotka's term. (If one denies the latter possibility as well as the former, then what's the point of education?) The argument has here been stated in the context of the population problem, but it applies equally well to any instance in which society appeals to an individual exploiting a commons to restrain himself for the general good-by means of his conscience. To make such an appeal is to set up a selective system that works toward the elimination of conscience from the race.

(7) Pathogenic Effects of Conscience

The long-term disadvantage of an appeal to conscience should be enough to condemn it; but has serious disadvantages as well. If we ask a man who is exploiting a commons to desist "in the name of conscience," what are we saying to him? What does he hear?-not only at the moment but also in the wee small hours of the night when, half asleep, he remembers not merely the words we used but also the nonverbal communication cues we gave him unawares? Sooner or later, consciously or subconsciously, he senses that he has received two communications, and that they are contradictory: (i) (intended communication) "If you don't do as we ask, we will openly condemn you for not acting like a responsible citizen"; (ii) (the unintended communication) "If you *do* behave as we ask, we will secretly condemn you for a simpleton who can be shamed into standing aside while the rest of us exploit the commons."

Everyman then is caught in what Bateson has called a "double bind." Bateson and his co-workers have made a plausible case for viewing the double bind as an important causative factor in the genesis of schizophrenia[16]. The double bind may not always be so damaging, but it always endangers the mental health of anyone to whom it is applied. "A bad conscience," said Nietzsche, "is a kind of illness."

To conjure up a conscience in others is tempting to anyone who wishes to extend his control beyond the legal limits. Leaders at the highest level succumb to this temptation. Has any President during the past generation failed to call on labor unions to moderate voluntarily their demands for higher wages, or to steel companies to honor voluntary guidelines on prices? I can recall none. The rhetoric used on such occasions is designed to produce feelings of guilt in non-cooperators.

For centuries it was assumed without proof that guilt was a valuable, perhaps even an indispensable, ingredient of the civilized life. Now, in this post-Freudian world, we doubt it.

Paul Goodman speaks from the modern point of view when he says: "No good has ever come from feeling guilty, neither intelligence, policy, nor compassion. The guilty do not pay attention to the object but only to themselves, and not even to their own interests, which might make sense, but to their anxieties"[17].

One does not have to be a professional psychiatrist to see the consequences of anxiety. We in the Western world are just emerging from a dreadful two-centuries-long Dark Ages of Eros that was sustained partly by prohibition laws, but perhaps more effectively by the anxiety-generating mechanisms of education. Alex Comfort has told the story well in *The Anxiety Makers*[18]; it is not a pretty one.

Since proof is difficult, we may even concede that the results of anxiety may sometimes, from certain points of view, be desirable. The larger question we should ask is whether, as a matter of policy, we should ever encourage the use of a technique the tendency (if not the intention) of which is psychologically pathogenic. We hear much talk these days of responsible parenthood; the coupled words are incorporated into the titles of some organizations devoted to birth control. Some people have proposed massive propaganda campaigns to instill responsibility into the nation's (or the world's) breeders. But what is the meaning of the word responsibility in this context? Is it not merely a synonym for the word conscience? When we use the word responsibility in the absence of substantial sanctions are we not trying to browbeat a free man in a commons into acting against his own interest? Responsibility is a verbal counterfeit for a substantial *quid pro quo*. It is an attempt to get something for nothing.

If the word responsibility is to be used at all, I suggest that it be in the sense Charles Frankel uses it[19]. "Responsibility," says this philosopher, "is the product of definite social arrangements." Notice that Frankel calls for social arrangements--not propaganda.

(8) Mutual Coercion, Mutually Agreed Upon

The social arrangements that produce responsibility are arrangements that create coercion, of some sort. Consider bank-robbing. The man who takes money from a bank acts as if the bank were a commons. How do we prevent such action? Certainly not by trying to control his behavior solely by a verbal appeal to his sense of responsibility, Rather than rely on propaganda we follow Frankel's lead and insist that a bank is not a commons; we seek the definite social arrangements that will keep it from becoming a commons. That we thereby infringe on the freedom of would-be robbers we neither deny nor regret.

The morality of bank-robbing is particularly easy to understand because we accept complete prohibition of this activity. We are willing to say "Thou shalt not rob banks," without providing for exceptions. But temperance also can be created by coercion. Taxing is a good coercive device. To keep downtown shoppers temperate in their use of parking space we introduce parking meters for short periods, and traffic fines for longer ones. We need not actually forbid a citizen to park as long as he wants to; we need merely make it increasingly expensive for him to do so. Not prohibition, but carefully biased options are what we offer him. A Madison Avenue man might call this persuasion; I prefer the greater candor of the word coercion.

Coercion is a dirty word to most liberals now, but it need not forever be so. As with the four-letter words, its dirtiness can be cleansed away by exposure to the light, by saying it over and over without apology or embarrassment. To many, the word coercion implies arbitrary decisions of distant and irresponsible bureaucrats; but this is not a necessary part of its meaning. The only kind of coercion I recommend is mutual coercion, mutually agreed upon by the majority of the people affected.

To say that we mutually agree to coercion is not to say that we are required to enjoy it, or even to pretend we enjoy it. Who enjoys taxes? We all grumble about them. But we accept compulsory taxes because we recognize that voluntary taxes would favor the conscienceless. We institute and (grumblingly) support taxes and other coercive devices to escape the horror of the commons.

An alternative to the commons need not be perfectly just to be preferable. With real estate and other material goods, the alternative we have chosen is the institution of private property coupled with legal inheritance. Is this system perfectly just? As a genetically trained biologist I deny that it is. It seems to me that, if there are to be differences in individual inheritance, legal possession should be perfectly correlated with biological inheritance--that those who are biologically more fit to be the custodians of property and power should legally inherit more. But genetic recombination continually makes a mockery of the doctrine of "like father, like son" implicit in our laws of legal inheritance. An idiot can inherit millions, and a trust fund can keep his estate intact. We must admit that our legal system of private property plus inheritance is unjust--but we put up with it because we are not convinced, at the moment, that anyone has invented a better system. The alternative of the commons is too horrifying to contemplate. Injustice is preferable to total ruin.

It is one of the peculiarities of the warfare between reform and the status quo that it is thoughtlessly governed by a double standard. Whenever a reform measure is proposed it is often defeated when its opponents triumphantly discover a flaw in it. As Kingsley Davis has pointed out,[20] worshippers of the status quo sometimes imply that no reform is possible without unanimous agreement, an implication contrary to historical fact. As nearly as I can make out, automatic rejection of proposed reforms is based on one of two unconscious assumptions: (i) that the status quo is perfect; or (ii) that the choice we face is between reform and no action; if the proposed reform is imperfect, we presumably should take no action at all, while we wait for a perfect proposal.

But we can never do nothing. That which we have done for thousands of years is also action. It also produces evils. Once we are aware that status quo is action, we can then compare its discoverable advantages and disadvantages with the predicted advantages and disadvantages of the proposed reform, discounting as best we can for our lack of experience. On the basis of such a comparison, we can make a rational decision which will not involve the unworkable assumption that only perfect systems are tolerable.

(9) Recognition of Necessity

Perhaps the simplest summary of this analysis of man's population problems is this: the commons, if justifiable at all, is justifiable only under conditions of low-population density. As the human population has increased, the commons has had to be abandoned in one aspect after another. First we abandoned the commons in food gathering, enclosing farm land and restricting pastures and hunting and fishing areas. These restrictions are still not complete throughout the world.

Somewhat later we saw that the commons as a place for waste disposal would also have to be abandoned. Restrictions on the disposal of domestic sewage are widely accepted in the Western world; we are still struggling to close the commons to pollution by automobiles, factories, insecticide sprayers, fertilizing operations, and atomic energy installations.

In a still more embryonic state is our recognition of the evils of the commons in matters of pleasure. There is almost no restriction on the propagation of sound waves in the public medium. The shopping public is assaulted with mindless music, without its consent. Our government is paying out billions of dollars to create supersonic transport which will disturb 50,000 people for every one person who is whisked from coast to coast 3 hours faster. Advertisers muddy the airwaves of radio and television and pollute the view of travelers. We are a long way from outlawing the commons in matters of pleasure. Is this because our Puritan inheritance makes us view pleasure as something of a sin, and pain (that is, the pollution of advertising) as the sign of virtue?

Every new enclosure of the commons involves the infringement of somebody's personal liberty. Infringements made in the distant past are accepted because no contemporary complains of a loss. It is the newly proposed infringements that we vigorously oppose; cries of "rights" and "freedom" fill the air. But what does "freedom" mean? When men mutually agreed to pass laws against robbing, mankind became freer, not less so. Individuals locked into the logic of the commons are free only to bring on universal ruin; once they see the necessity of mutual coercion, they become free to pursue other goals. I believe it was Hegel who said, "Freedom is the recognition of necessity."

The most important aspect of necessity that we must now recognize, is the necessity of abandoning the commons in breeding. No technical solution can rescue us from the misery of overpopulation. Freedom to breed will bring ruin to all. At the moment, to avoid hard decisions many of us are tempted to propagandize for conscience and responsible parenthood. The temptation must be resisted, because an appeal to independently acting consciences selects for the disappearance of all conscience in the long run, and an increase in anxiety in the short.

The only way we can preserve and nurture other and more precious freedoms is by relinquishing the freedom to breed, and that very soon. "Freedom is the recognition of necessity"--and it is the role of education to reveal to all the necessity of abandoning the freedom to breed. Only so, can we put an end to this aspect of the tragedy of the commons.

Section 2 South-To-North cooperation in Asia

(1) The Types of Economic Cooperation

In general, there are two types of regional cooperation: South-to-South cooperation means the regional cooperation among the developing countries. General speaking, South-to-South cooperation contains no element for success. There are some reasons as follows: a. because of their narrow domestic market, it is difficult for a developing country to absorb the goods imported from other member countries; b. it is very hard for them to form a close linkage through division of labor; harmonization of various policies of the developing countries is very difficult; c. there is a serious trade diversion effect existing in the South-to-South cooperation. South-to-North cooperation refers to the regional cooperation between the developing countries and the developed countries. By participating in the regional cooperation, the developing countries could accelerate their own industrialization process through the vertical division of labor shared with the developed countries.

Thus, to the developing countries, a regional cooperative grouping with the rich countries is preferred to South-to-South integration: a. it helps the developing countries to expand export, b. it helps to attract foreign investment from the developed countries, c. it promotes technology transfer from the advanced countries to the developing countries. It also benefits the developed countries. By cutting tariff level and providing larger market access to the developing countries, the developed countries can get the developing countries' cooperation in exchange in the non-tradable fields including labor standardization, intellectual property, migrant and security etc.

APT economic cooperation contains not only the element of South-to-South cooperation but also the element of South-to-North cooperation. ASEAN-China cooperation could be classified as the former one, while Japan-ASEAN, Korea-ASEAN, or Japan-China, Korea-China cooperation will be the latter ones.[21] These two types of cooperation coexist and interact in the process of East Asian cooperation and both of them exert great influence upon the whole regional economic growth. With a relatively small domestic market, Korea is just playing the role as a coordinator. And so, we will only discuss the impact of the tri-party cooperation upon the East Asian economic growth, namely the cooperation among ASEAN, Japan and China.

(2) Cooperation between ASEAN and China

According to the analysis, due to its inherent weaknesses, few South-to-South cooperation gets a success. However, in the case of ASEAN-China cooperation, China is a huge developing country with dramatically rising economic scale, a vast domestic market, and multi-layered economic structure. Some industries and some coastal areas in China are relatively advanced, which makes China-ASEAN cooperation appear dual-natured. Viewing the cooperation as a whole, it belongs to South-to-South one, however, if viewing the certain parts of it, it may turn to be South-to-North cooperation. In my opinion, this is the real foundation for the future successful cooperation between China and ASEAN.

Because of the similarity in their economic development level and trade structure, most of time they are in a fierce rivalry in the international market, for this reason, it is difficult for both of them to enhance their bilateral relations. However, China-ASEAN FTA opened a great opportunity for ASEAN members to get access to China's market. And since then, Sino-ASEAN economic and trade relations improved considerably. According to the statistics of Chinese Ministry of Commerce, from January to October of 2004, bilateral trade amounted to 84.61 billion US dollars. It is worth of notice that China's import from ASEAN reached 51.04 billion dollars its export to ASEAN was only 33. 57 billion US dollars. So China's trade deficit with ASEAN during this period was 17. 47 billion US dollars, this was not a small number. China's imports from ASEAN not only included raw materials such as agricultural products, mineral products etc, but also included a great number of intermediate products like electronic components, parts. China's import structure from ASEAN has been enhanced.[22] The rising trade deficit on China's side proves that China is increasingly becoming a main consumer of ASEAN's products. At present, ASEAN member countries are taking more export to China as an engine for their economic growth. In a few years of continuously being the most important manufacturing center of the world, China will import more and more raw material, fuel and intermediated industrial products, and ASEAN will be an important source of China's imports.

Moreover, with the process of China-ASEAN FTA getting fast, ASEAN's export to China will reach a higher growth rate it means that China's deficit will also get a rise, which will to some extent offset the unfavorable influence resulting from the investment diversion away from ASEAN to China during the post-crisis period. China, as a potential market of 1.3 billion population and ASEAN as a potential market of 500 million population their combined market size is huge, therefore, China-ASEAN cooperation will boost East Asian future economic growth as a whole.

Section 3 Monetary policy of China and other Asian countries

(1) Costs and Benefits of the Currency Peg

In the 1950s and 1960s, although China pegged to the U.S. dollar and then to the British pound, the exchange rate had little relevance for trade and resource flows, the vast majority of which were directly controlled. With the breakdown of Bretton Woods, the country's single currency peg was then replaced by a broad basket. In 1981 China devalued what had become a massively overvalued rate and temporarily introduced a separate, so-called official rate for non-trade (mainly remittances and tourism).[23] A de facto multiple exchange rate system was introduced in 1985-6 when the authorities sanctioned a formal secondary market for foreign exchange (on which foreign currency retained by exports could be traded). In 1994 China unified the RMB at the then prevailing rate to the dollar of 8.2770, which then appreciated very modestly to 8.27 in 1995, where it then remained (see Figure5-1). In the second half of the 1990s, as part of developing a system of direct monetary control, the growth of the money stock began replacing credit ceilings as the intermediate target of the PBOC, and a unified inter-bank money market began operating in Shanghai. The PBOC then introduced open market operations, which have now played a role in monetary management for more than five years. Qualified commercial banks and other financial institutions are authorized to trade treasury securities and to quote buy and sell rates for foreign exchange within a plus and minus 0.3 per cent band.[24] In practice the PBOC has intervened to limit actual fluctuations to plus or minus 0.1 per cent. (See Figure 5-2)

Average Daily RMB/US$ Exchange Rate

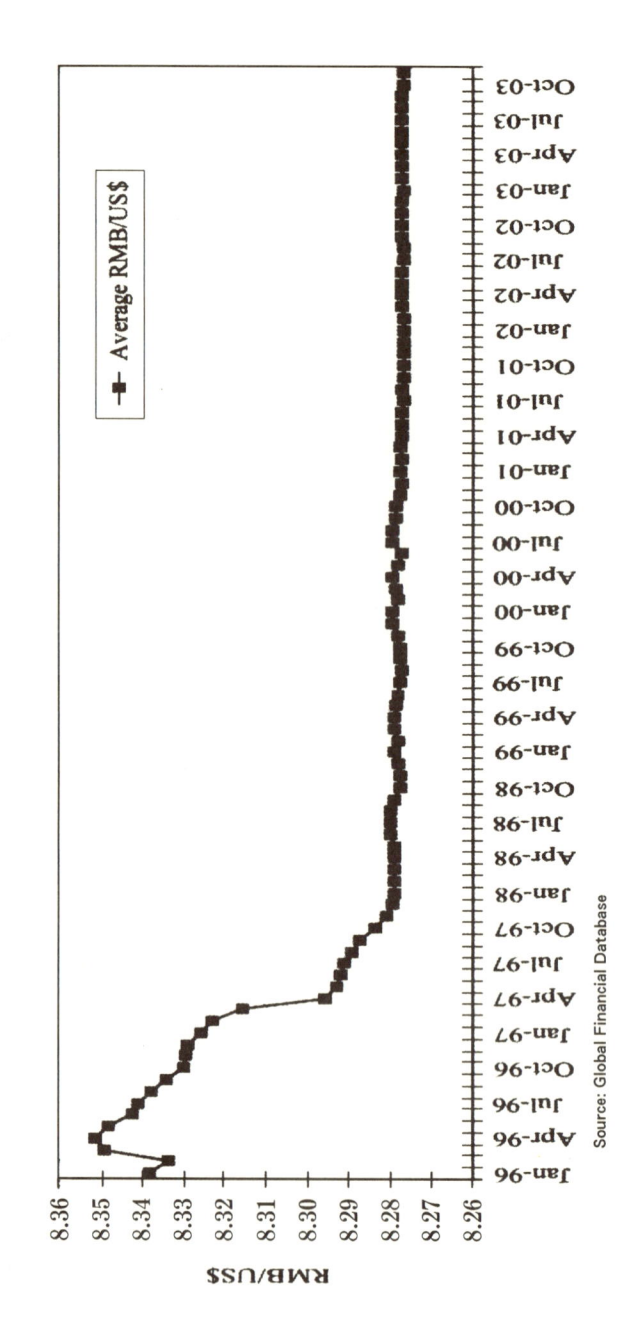

Figure 5-1

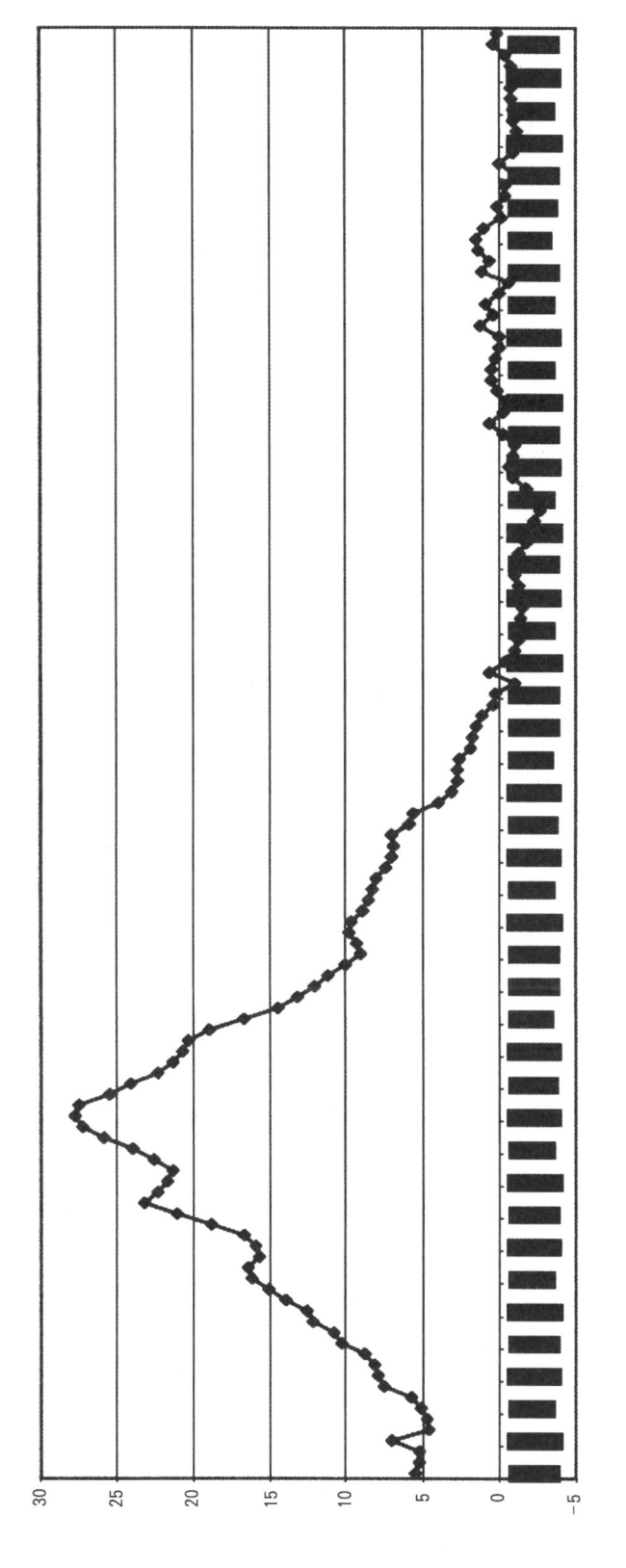

China's Inflation calculated from Y-o-Y change of CPI

Source: IFS

Figure 5-2

Benefits of the peg

The pegged exchange rate is valued for the stimulus it provides to export-led growth. In adopting the Asian model of export-led growth supported by a competitively valued exchange rate, China is pursuing a strategy previously followed by Japan, South Korea, Taiwan, Singapore, Thailand and other Asian economies. In recent years, exports have been far and away the fastest growing component of Chinese GDP, rising at rates in excess of 20 per cent per annum. China's utility as an export platform is also a key attraction for the foreign direct investment that has been so important for the country's economic development.

No doubt exchange rate stability eases planning and eliminates what is at least a minor inconvenience for multinational companies and, more importantly, for the domestic private enterprises that play a growing role in the country's export drive. But econometric studies of the impact of exchange rate variability on foreign trade and investment detect at best small effects.[25] The rapid growth of Chinese exports and the incentive for foreigners to engage in direct investment reflect more than just the level of the exchange rate. Reform in China and the country's entry into the World Trade Organization coincided with a rise in global outsourcing made possible by advances in information and communications technology. China is an attractive locale for outsourced production because of its abundant supplies of labor (including, increasingly, skilled labor), long coastline, and large potential market. A modest change in the level of the exchange rate and/or a permanent shift to a somewhat higher level of exchange rate variability might moderate export growth slightly in the short run, but they would do nothing to alter these favorable fundamentals.

Multinationals, for their part, can protect themselves from the effects of exchange rate variability by building diversified portfolios of production facilities and by sourcing from a number of different countries.[26] Multinational companies' joint venture partners do not enjoy the same diversification (although we are now beginning to see some Chinese companies going abroad), but if temporary appreciation of the exchange rate causes them financial difficulty they can still obtain assistance from their joint-venture partners. They are unlikely to be liquidity constrained, in other words. There is thus no reason why a more flexible renminbi should make life significantly more difficult for such companies.

Note that we are talking here about the majority of Chinese exports and two thirds of recent export growth. The share of China's total exports accounted for by foreign owned enterprises has risen from 28 per cent in 1993 to 41 per cent in 1996 and 54 per cent 2003. (See Figure 5-3) In effect, 65 per cent of the increase in China's exports over this period came from multinationals' China subsidiaries and joint ventures. For a country where foreign investment enterprises and joint ventures account for the bulk of exports, the impact

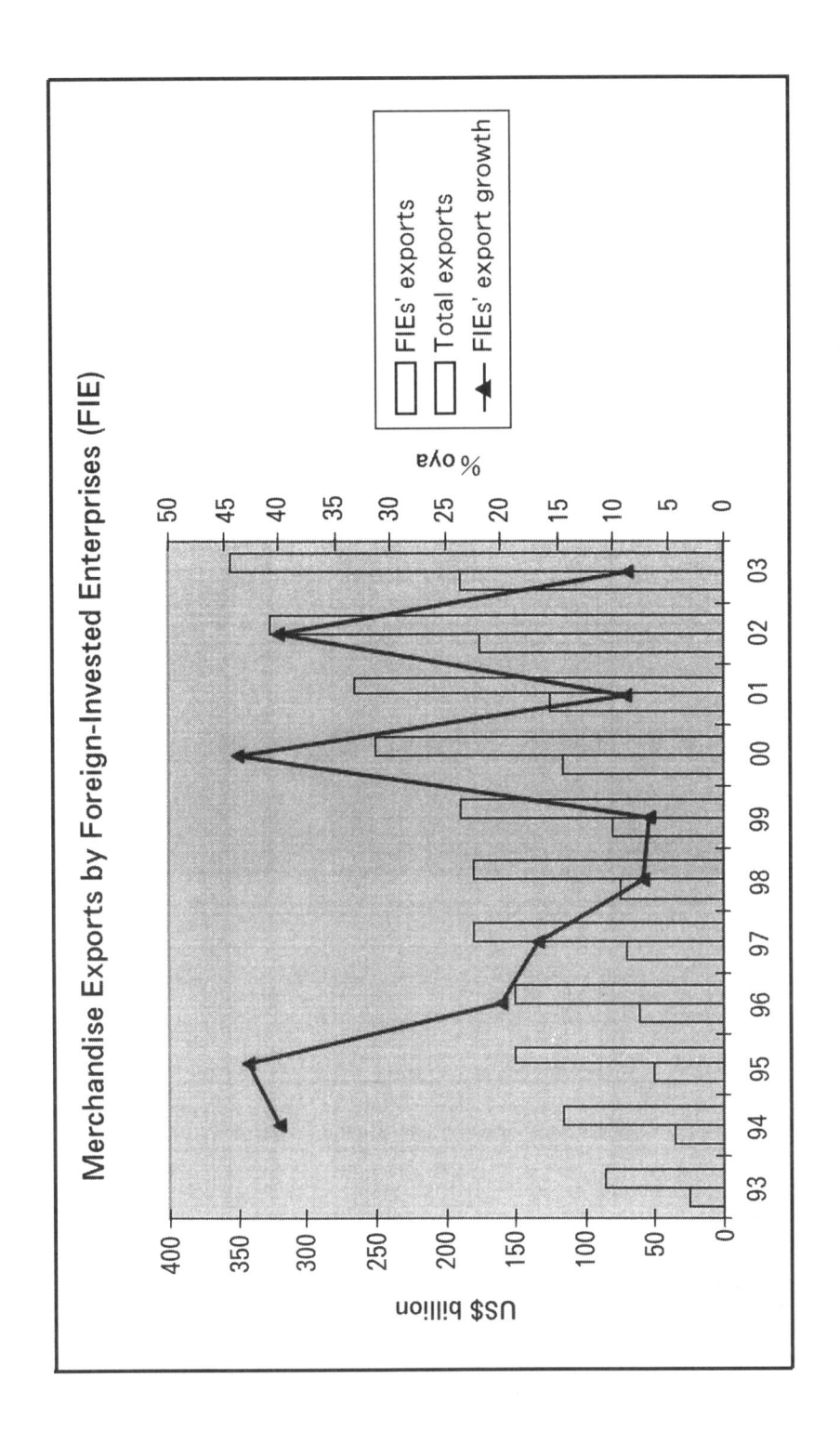

Merchandise Exports by Foreign-Invested Enterprises (FIE)

Source: Zheng 2003b.

Figure 5-3

on exports of a slightly more volatile exchange rate should be relatively weak.

The main place to worry about the impact of greater exchange rate variability is private domestically owned firms, which have been allowed to export directly since 1999 (instead of having to go through state-owned trade companies). These enterprises are least able to protect themselves from exchange rate changes. If currency appreciation causes them financial distress, they will have to seek help from the banking system. One can reasonably question whether China's banking system is up to the task - in particular whether its credit evaluation procedures are adequate for distinguishing temporary from chronic problems among its clients. But the impact should not be exaggerated. The share of private domestically owned firms in total exports is still less than 10 per cent.[27] And, insofar as a large share of export content takes the form of imported components even for private domestically owned firms, changes in the exchange rate affect both costs and revenues in the same direction and therefore do not give rise to severe financial difficulties.

Costs of the peg

None of this is to deny that a more flexible exchange rate will complicate life for private domestically owned firms. But the new regime will also have significant benefits. In particular, the PBOC will be better able to limit procyclicality of money and credit. Under a pegged rate, positive shocks to productivity and growth lead to positive shocks to supplies of money and credit. Any incipient rise in domestic interest rates, which would damp down the surge in economic activity, is at least partially offset by capital inflows or declining outflows. Chinese officials tend to deny the existence of this link, since the country has controls limiting the ability of banks and corporations to arbitrage domestic and foreign interest rates. If the authorities wish to limit the rate of growth of bank credit and raise the level of interest rates relative to those prevailing abroad, they can simply issue sterilization bills, thereby sopping up the additional domestic liquidity, and issue directives to the banks instructing them to lend less, as they did in 2004. But as the capital account grows more porous, tightening domestic credit conditions by selling short-term bills and three-year sterilization bonds just strengthens the tendency for capital to flow in. While the PBOC has been working hard to sterilize capital inflows, it has been only partially successful. And as the Chinese economy is further liberalized, there develop an increasing number of additional channels, other than the banking system through which capital can flow in from abroad and have an impact on the domestic economy. Foreign multinationals can bring in additional funds and use them to purchase apartments as well as engage in industrial investment. Overseas Chinese can engage in similar transactions while on holiday on the mainland. Foreign banks are increasingly able to engage in such transactions as they gain a foothold courtesy of China's WTO membership.

Recent studies have confirmed the existence of a surprisingly strong link between monetary conditions in China and the United States. Ouyang and Rajan (2005) estimate the offset coefficient (the impact of a change in net domestic assets on net foreign assets) by two-stage least squares on data starting in 1995, obtaining a coefficient of 0.5, indicating that about half of any domestic monetary impulse is offset by induced capital flows. It is safe to assume that this coefficient has been trending upward over time. Cheung, Chinn and Fujii (2003) analyze monetary and financial linkages between China and the United States (as well as Hong Kong and Taiwan) over the period 1996-2002, taking the magnitude of the real interest differential as a measure of integration. They report that the real interest differential trends downward over time 8 and "surprisingly positive" evidence of integration with the United States. Decomposing the real interest differential into the uncovered interest differential and the relative purchasing power parity differential, they find that a downward trend in the former is mainly responsible for the shrinking real interest differential vis-a-vis the United States. The persistence of these differentials confirms that Chinese capital controls continue to bite, but their declining magnitude at the same time suggests that financial integration is growing increasingly tight, limiting Chinese monetary autonomy so long as the currency remains pegged. The result is to amplify the economy's boom and bust cycles. The $35.8 billion of non-FDI capital inflows received by China in 2003 (amounting to 2.7 per cent of GDP), at the same time the economy was booming ahead, provides clear evidence of the linkage. In this episode, property-market arbitrage has been the mechanism linking domestic and foreign financial conditions. The expectation is that property prices in Shanghai will eventual converge to those in Hong Kong and Taiwan. Low interest rates in these other markets, which have sustained property price increases there, also thereby fuel price increases in China. When the authorities try to tighten up on bank lending to the property market, funds for real estate speculation instead flow in from abroad, as foreign investment enterprises divert authorized inflows into property purchases, as overseas Chinese repatriate their funds, and through a variety of other mechanisms.

Another manifestation of the same problem is the growing tendency for Chinese commercial banks to balk at buying (at prevailing interest rates) the bills that the central bank issues in its effort to sterilize the impact of financial inflows on the domestic money supply (see the discussion in the *Financial Times*, 30 December 2003, p.10). The more that state banks are commercialized, the less will become the scope for using direct pressure to guide bank lending, and thus the rate of growth of the broad money supply. The very strong correlation between M29 and foreign reserves since late 2001 is additional evidence that inflows have not been fully sterilized and instead have found their way into the banking system (Ong 2004). Pegging the currency therefore limits the scope for moving to a market-based monetary policy since it limits the extent to which monetary conditions can move independently. In the present context, this shows up in rising real estate, commodity and shipping prices. A weaker dollar does not help: effective (trade-weighted) depreciation and rising import prices are not helpful when the authorities' task is to combat inflation.

The peg also prevents the authorities from moving to a regime in which interest rates are used to allocate credit. Indiscriminate property lending is again the most obvious manifestation of the consequences. Property lending has been expanding by 25 per cent per annum, causing investment in real estate to rise 30 per cent year on year. To date, property prices have risen somewhat less rapidly, reflecting the elasticity of the supply response, although there are signs that the property market is heating up; at the time of writing real estate prices in Shanghai are reportedly rising at a 30 per cent annual clip. Another manifestation of this resource misallocation is the government's massive accumulation of foreign reserves, resources that are disproportionately held in low-yielding foreign government securities rather than being devoted to high yielding private investment, or for that matter desperately sought-after domestic consumption. These are more signs that the authorities' inability to tailor domestic financial conditions to local needs results in a misallocation of resources.

Then there are the implications for the banking system. In 2002, a period of unusually low interest rates in the United States, bank deposits in China rose by more than 15 per cent. Given the growing reluctance of the commercial banks, as noted above, to purchase the bills used by the authorities to sterilize the effects of financial inflows, bank credit surged by 17 per 10 cent. This was unhelpful in a period when questions were already being raised about the quality of investment and the sustainability of rapid growth.[28] It is inconsistent with efforts to raise bank loan standards since, other things equal, a larger volume of loans is an indication of a decline in their quality on the margin.. It has encouraged the explosive growth of property lending; consumer loans, of which over 80 per cent are home mortgages, now constitute 11 per cent of total bank loans. They accounted for almost 25 per cent of total loan growth in 2004 despite the imposition of stricter controls on mortgage loans (Ng 2005). This creates vulnerabilities for the banking system that will be disturbingly familiar to observers of other countries.

The expedients used by the authorities have not been very effective at moderating these pressures. Increasing reserve requirements for commercial banks puts upward pressure on interest rates but only attract additional capital inflows, given the permeability of the capital account. This is evident in the acceleration in the growth of base money following the first rise in reserve requirements. The same is true of the contractionary open market operations implemented through sales of central bank bills on the inter-bank market. A radical tightening of capital controls is the one guaranteed way of reconciling domestic monetary autonomy with maintenance of the currency peg. But the authorities have been moving in the other way; they are committed to further opening the capital account prior to moving to a more flexible exchange rate. Beginning on Oct 1, 2003, they authorized Chinese residents to purchase foreign exchange worth U.S. $3,000 for each trip abroad, up from the previous limit of $2,000. (The amount for those who stay abroad for half a year or longer is an even higher $5,000.) They have also liberalized restrictions on the ability of Chinese residents to enter the Hong Kong stock market. They have loosened requirements for exporting enterprises to surrender their foreign exchange earnings. They have allowed local companies involved in international project contracting and labor services to keep foreign exchange income from the previous year instead of having to surrender it to the authorities. They have relaxed restrictions on the ability of Chinese companies to undertake direct investments abroad. They are allowing Chinese insurance companies to add foreign assets to their investment portfolios. They are considering a Qualified Domestic Institutional Investor Program that would permit Chinese institutions to invest in stock and bond markets abroad. Because of the unsatisfied demand for portfolio diversification on the part of Chinese residents, it is hoped that such measures will encourage a modest capital outflow and lead to somewhat tighter conditions on domestic financial markets. But the same channels that convey outflows can also convey inflows. If anything, the Chinese authorities have encouraged this process by relaxing restrictions on selected capital inflows at the same time that they have attempted to facilitate outflows (Zhang 2003a). For example, they have signaled a readiness to authorize renminbi-denominated bond issuance by the International Finance Corporation and the Asian Development Bank. On the eve of the Communist Party Conference in 2002, they agreed to implement the Qualified Foreign Investor Program, which allows selected foreign investors access to China's domestic equity and debt markets. Note that foreigners engaged in portfolio investment in principle have the option of repatriating their investments on demand.

All this means that the measures taken by the authorities do little to insulate domestic markets from global financial conditions. If anything they have the opposite effect. This has hindered efforts to raise lending standards in the banking system and heightened the fragility of the currency peg, as evident most recently in the massive capital inflows motivated by expectations that it will not be possible for the authorities to maintain the peg indefinitely.

(2) What Kind of New Regime?

Assume that the case for a change in China's exchange rate is granted. What then should be the nature of the adjustment and the form of the new regime?

A Step Revaluation

A substantial one-time revaluation would diminish protectionist pressure in the United States. It is also an obvious way of cooling off the Chinese economy and fighting inflationary pressure. But a step revaluation would not address the other problems with the peg. Once prices and costs adjust, earlier problems would simply recur. The authorities would have acquired no greater ability to tailor financial and foreign-exchange-market conditions to domestic needs. And revaluing once, by undermining the belief that the level of the exchange rate is the linchpin of policy, will encourage expectations that the authorities might revalue again. This will only worsen the problem of speculative capital flows, in turn amplifying the procyclicality of monetary conditions. To defend the new level of the exchange rate, the authorities will have to deny that they have any intention of revaluing again, even if domestic and international disequilibria become relatively severe. Every system of pegged but adjustable exchange rates has grown increasingly rigid and unadjustable over time, as the authorities have been forced to reassure the markets that their early resort to exchange rate changes will not be repeated. Insofar as China's capital account will inevitably become more porous, the problem will worsen. For all these reasons, a one-time adjustment would only compound the exit problem.[29]

Another problem with a step revaluation is that there will be serious fallout if the 13 authorities get the magnitude wrong. A revaluation that is too small will only excite expectations of a further revaluation in the not very distant future, which will worsen the problem of speculative inflows and procyclical monetary conditions. One of the first rules of currency policy is not to make administered changes in exchange rates too small; the problem in the present case is knowing what too small is.

At the same time, a one-time revaluation that is too large could unnecessarily slow the growth of the Chinese economy. Garber (2003) estimates that a 10 per cent revaluation would destroy (or prevent the creation of) half a million industrial jobs. Since the change in the exchange rate would presumably be one time, job creation would resume subsequently. But even a temporary slowdown in urban job creation could fan political unrest, thereby undermining investor confidence. Some estimates put China's unemployment rate at as high as 15 per cent of the labor force; this means that dimming hopes of future employment cannot be taken lightly as a political matter (given that only one in seven members of the labor force has any form of unemployment insurance).[30]

Thus, the fundamental problem with the step revaluation strategy is knowing the appropriate amount by which to revalue. Estimates of the extent of the renminbi's undervaluation are all over the map. For example, relative to its average between the middle of 1996 and the middle of 2002, the RMB is undervalued on a real effective basis (weighted relative to

Real Effective Exchange Rate

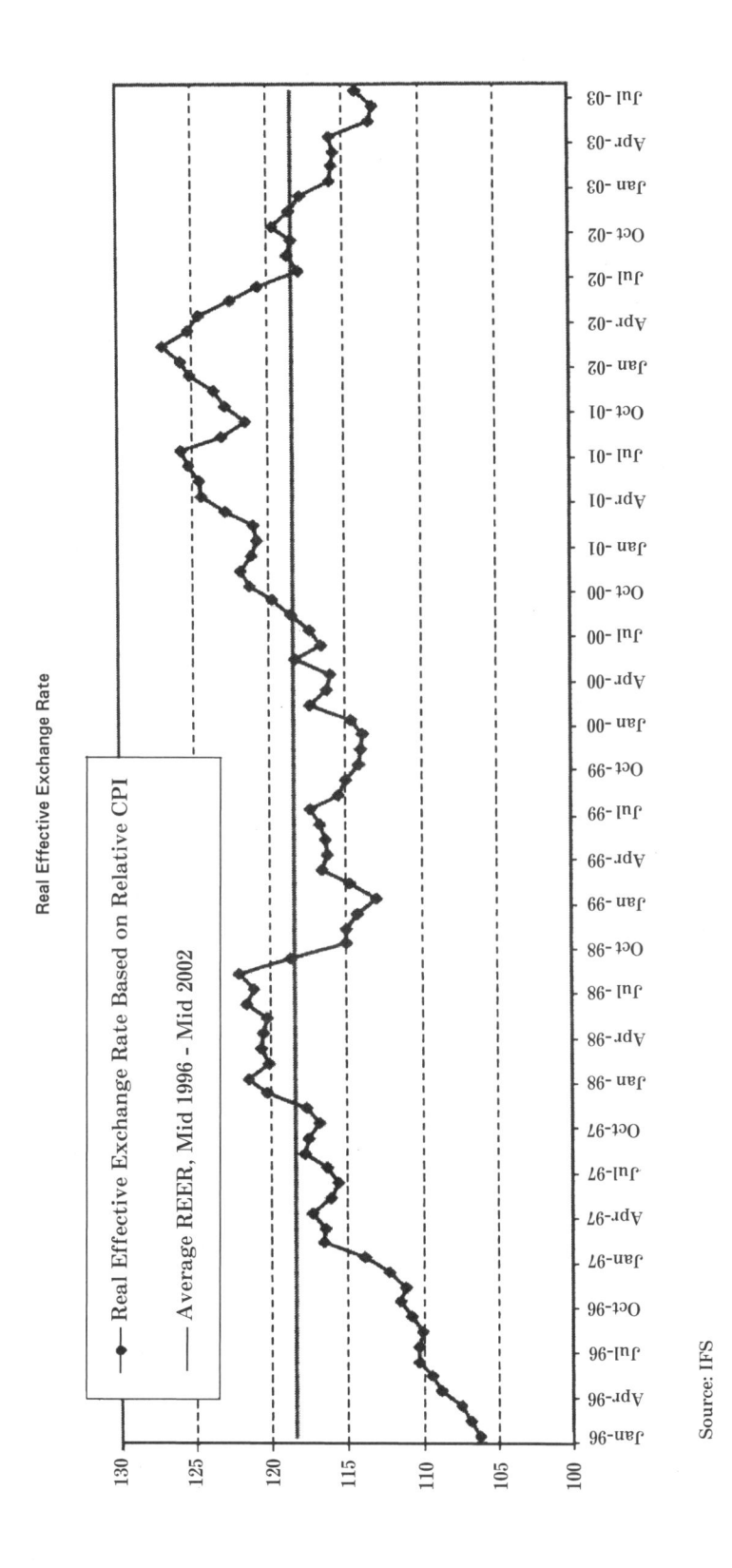

— Real Effective Exchange Rate Based on Relative CPI
— Average REER, Mid 1996 – Mid 2002

Source: IFS

Figure 5-4

the relative labor costs of its principal trading partners) by only about 5 per cent. (See Figure 5-4) This estimate is consistent with the conclusions of IMF Executive Directors in November 2003 that "there is no substantial evidence that the remnimbi is undervalued..." (IMF 2003). Alternatively, the revaluation needed to balance the current account adjusted for long-term capital inflows is estimated to be on the order of 15 to 25 per cent (see for example Goldstein 2003 or Merrill Lynch 2004). These estimates strike me as too high. Only under very optimistic scenarios will foreign direct investment inflows continue indefinitely at the present rapid pace. Currently, much of the capital inflow into China is speculative, motivated by expectations of revaluation. Once a modest revaluation occurs and especially if the authorities then move to a managed float, introducing a two-way bet, those speculative inflows will subside.

A Step Revaluation with a Shift to a Basket Peg

The step revaluation could be taken as an occasion to replace the dollar peg with a broader basket that includes not just the dollar but also the euro, the yen, and the currencies of China's other principal trade partners. Retaining the peg but just changing its composition would presumably do little to shake confidence. Because the RMB would no longer rise and fall in lockstep with the dollar, its movement in times of dollar depreciation would no longer cause such difficulties for other regions, such as Europe.

Because monetary conditions would now be imported not just from the United States but also from other countries, those monetary conditions would presumably be more stable.[31] Insofar as the sources of imported inputs and the destinations of manufactured exports are growing increasingly diverse, stability vis-a-vis a basket as opposed to the dollar would simplify the country's international transactions overall.

But simply shifting to a basket would not address the other problems created by the maintenance of a currency peg. In particular it would not enhance the ability of the Chinese authorities to tailor monetary conditions to domestic needs.

A Step Revaluation with a Later Shift to a Float

This is the essence of Goldstein and Lardy's (2003) proposal for a two-step adjustment. In the first, step a one-time 15-25 per cent revaluation would be accompanied by only a very slight widening of the fluctuation band slightly. This would then be followed down the road by a shift to a freer float, but only after the financial sector had been strengthened and the capital account had been further liberalized. Floating would allow the currency to adjust to future developments: the exchange rate could adjust upward if Chinese productivity and exports continued to surge ahead, or it could adjust downward if the economy cooled and/ or problems developed in the financial sector. Delaying the shift to a freer float until the banking sector was restructured would ensure that exchange rate fluctuations did not give rise to serious financial problems. Delaying it until the capital account had been further liberalized would mean that the foreign exchange market would be more liquid and stabilizing capital flows would be forthcoming. The appropriateness of a step revaluation of the exact magnitude proposed by the authors can be questioned for all the reasons enumerated above. In addition, all the other drawbacks of the peg will remain if the shift to significantly greater flexibility is delayed. Indeed, if the authorities announce that the step revaluation will be followed by further exchange rate adjustments (presumably in the direction of further revaluation), they may worsen the problem of destabilizing capital inflows (relative to a benchmark in which there was uncertainty about the direction of future exchange rate movements). Moving immediately to a managed float would not create this same danger, since a managed float introduces the possibility of two-way movements in the exchange rate, making it less likely that market participants will all line up on one side of the market. In addition, Goldstein and Lardy's rationales for delaying the transition to floating and 16 therefore for distinguishing the two steps can be questioned. A first rationale is that the Chinese banking system will be unable to cope with the additional stresses of floating. It is undoubtedly true that rapid capital account liberalization would create additional dangers for financial stability. Big banks with extensive nonperforming loans would have an incentive to borrow offshore as a way of gambling for redemption. Knowing that the authorities regarded them as too big to fail, their foreign counterparts would be tempted to lend. But my argument is not for more rapid capital account liberalization; it is for greater exchange rate flexibility. Most advocates of greater exchange rate flexibility do not also advocate the relaxation of restrictions on the ability of the banks to borrow offshore. To the contrary, they emphasize the need to strengthen supervision and regulation of the banking system and to retain capital account restrictions as a further form of prudential regulation.

Indeed, if continued tight regulation of the capital account prevents the banks from funding themselves offshore in foreign currency, while prudential supervision and regulation prevent them from making foreign-currency-denominated loans to firms in the non-traded goods sector, then there is no obvious reason why limited currency fluctuations should significantly compound the problems of the banks. In contrast to the situation in South Korea or Thailand in 1997, the banks have not been permitted to freely fund themselves offshore, in foreign currency; thus, they do not have significant currency mismatches. A substantial share of the banks' capital, recently replenished by the authorities, is nominally denominated in dollars, but this is a bookkeeping convention that is easily changed by officials to prevent them from suffering capital losses in the event of appreciation. The loans of the banking system are not all extended to export-oriented enterprises whose ability to repay would be most immediately cast into doubt by an appreciation of the currency. As shown in Figure

5-5, much of this lending is infrastructure credit, rural credit, and consumer credit. If a more flexible exchange rate allows the authorities to better tailor financial conditions to the economy's needs, moderating boom and bust cycles, then balance sheet risks would become easier to manage, not harder. The banking system would be stabilized so long as significant currency mismatches were avoided. None of this questions that the problems in China's banking system are serious. Estimates of nonperforming loans are on the order of 40-50 per cent of GDP. Cleaning up this mess should be an urgent priority. Chinese officials appreciate: thus, they have recapitalized two state banks and have unveiled an "incentive-based" approach to reform, in which success at meeting benchmarks is rewarded with further recapitalization and access to capital markets. But the problem will not be significantly compounded by a somewhat more flexible exchange rate, assuming that they continue to go slow on liberalizing the capital account and make progress in strengthening prudential oversight of the banks. In this sense, the banking-sector problem is not a valid argument for delaying the transition to a managed float. Nor is the fact that full capital account convertibility will not be implemented anytime soon. To be sure, full capital account liberalization will not be feasible until the banking system is cleaned up. But history is replete with examples of countries that have operated managed floats while retaining capital controls of one sort or another. One might point to European countries in the 1930s, or Japan in the 1970s, or Chile in the 1990s, or Brazil and India today.

Still, the idea that a more flexible exchange rate is only feasible once the capital account has been fully liberalized is widely asserted, in disregard of this evidence. One possible justification could be that the currency will be excessively volatile if international financial 18 transactions remain controlled. It will not be possible for most residents and foreigners to sell the renminbi when it appreciates temporarily or to buy it on the dip. And because the market is illiquid, its volatility will be greater.

This view assumes that financial speculation is stabilizing and minimizes the possibility of herd behavior and self-fulfilling dynamics like those emphasized in recent models of balance of payments crises. Both assumptions are questionable. This means that it is not obvious in practice that further opening of the capital account would reduce exchange rate volatility, other things equal. Moreover, this view ignores the fact that current account transactions also generate a supply and a demand for foreign exchange, the balance of which determines the equilibrium price of foreign currency. A look at the international economics textbooks of the 1960s and 1970s (when capital mobility was low) reveals a catalog of models in which exports generate a flow supply of foreign exchange and imports generate a flow demand. Most importantly, this view ignores that the central bank will remain an important provider of liquidity to the market. Even if the exchange rate is allowed somewhat more flexibility, under any plausible scenario it will still be heavily managed by the PBOC. The central bank will be buying the renminbi in response to temporary depreciations and selling it when the currency starts appreciating to an undesirable extent. The idea that floating should be delayed until the capital account is significantly liberalized in order to limit the currency's volatility would make sense if we were talking about a free float. But this is not something that almost anyone has in mind.[32] Rather, most observers have in mind a managed float where the central bank provides the liquidity that international financial markets cannot. The other rationale for delaying the transition until the capital account has been significantly liberalized is that capital controls prevent firms from using financial instruments to insulate themselves from the effects of currency fluctuations. Firms import inputs as part of the process of producing and selling exports; the absence of an onshore market in currency forwards and futures would prevent them from insuring themselves against unexpected currency fluctuations during the production process. Similarly, firms make capital investments now by borrowing domestic currency in order to build the capacity to export later; an unexpected change in the exchange rate that reduces the domestic-currency price of exports can wreak havoc with balance sheets unless the firms in question have foreign-currency liabilities, obtained on foreign financial markets or from foreign financial institutions presuming prudential limits on the currency mismatches of domestic financial institutions. Again, hedging currency exposure in this way will be impossible in the absence of capital account liberalization. I have already indicated reasons for not taking these arguments too far. The majority of Chinese exports are produced by multinational companies and their joint venture partners, who can self-insure against such risks. In addition, the central bank, by managing the float to prevent excessive fluctuations, will limit financial dislocations for exporters. The literature on "fear of floating" (e.g. Calvo and Reinhart 2002) points to precisely this desire to limit balance-sheet dislocations as an explanation for the prevalence of heavily managed floating in emerging markets.

Moving Now to a Managed Float

These arguments suggest that China should not wait to open its capital account before moving to a managed float. Precisely when to move to greater flexibility is a more difficult question; rigorous analyses of the optimal sequencing of capital account liberalization and exchange rate flexibility are few. Part of the problem is that the capital account regime is treated in the theoretical literature as a dichotomous variable, where in reality there is a continuum of stages of capital account openness' that range from fully closed to fully open. We know that a country with a fully closed capital account has good reason to peg its currency. Hedging opportunities for exporters and importers being nonexistent, flexibility would be disruptive. We also know that a country with a fully open capital account will want to move to some form of greater exchange rate flexibility, except in a few very exceptional cases (like the case of Hong Kong, discussed below). Indeed, authors like Fischer (2003) regard moving to managed flexibility as an essential precondition for full capital account liberalization. My own view is that capital account liberalization has gone far enough that China should move now to a more flexible exchange rate. The events of 2002-3 and econometric studies like Cheung, Chinn and Fujii (2003) suggest that the capital account has grown sufficiently porous to seriously limit the authorities' room for maneuver.[33] And, given the risks of attempting to reconcile a liberal capital account with a pegged exchange rate, going further in the direction of capital account liberalization before moving to greater currency flexibility would create more problems than it solves. In addition, experience suggests that when the capital account becomes moderately open, there is a spontaneous tendency for it to open further. Remaining controls weaken whether the authorities like it or not. Economically, opening some channels for capital flows creates additional avenues through which market participants can evade remaining restrictions.[34] Politically, allowing residents and foreigners to engage in some international financial transactions creates interest groups that lobby for the removal of restrictions on other such transactions. In China's case, the simple fact that the country is becoming more integrated with the global economy, leading to its accession to the World Trade Organization, creates obligations- such as national treatment for foreign banks - implying a more porous capital account. All these are reasons for the Chinese authorities not to delay in moving to a managed float Moving directly from the peg to a managed float will simplify the adjustment to the new regime. It will diminish the need to assume that the authorities somehow know the precise magnitude of any overvaluation. If the initial decision is to allow the currency to drift up by, say,

5 per cent, but this turns out to do too little to slow the accumulation of reserves and to prevent the economy from overheating, then the authorities can engage in further open market sales to push the exchange rate up a bit further. An initial adjustment that is too small does less to damage credibility, putting the authorities in an unsustainable position, when the new regime is a shift to a market determined exchange rate that can adjust to changing circumstances than when it is a hard-and-fast peg that will supposedly be set and held. Since the currency can appreciate as well as depreciate, speculators will be deterred by the existence of this two-way bet from all lining up on one side of the market, and the problem of anticipatory capital inflows will be less. If economic conditions change and market pressures cause the exchange rate to move, then the authorities can use that information and lean against the wind harder or softer depending on whether they see the change in conditions as temporary or permanent. Thus, shifting to a managed float does not relieve the authorities of the need to have a view of the appropriate level or range for the exchange

Bank Lending by Sector

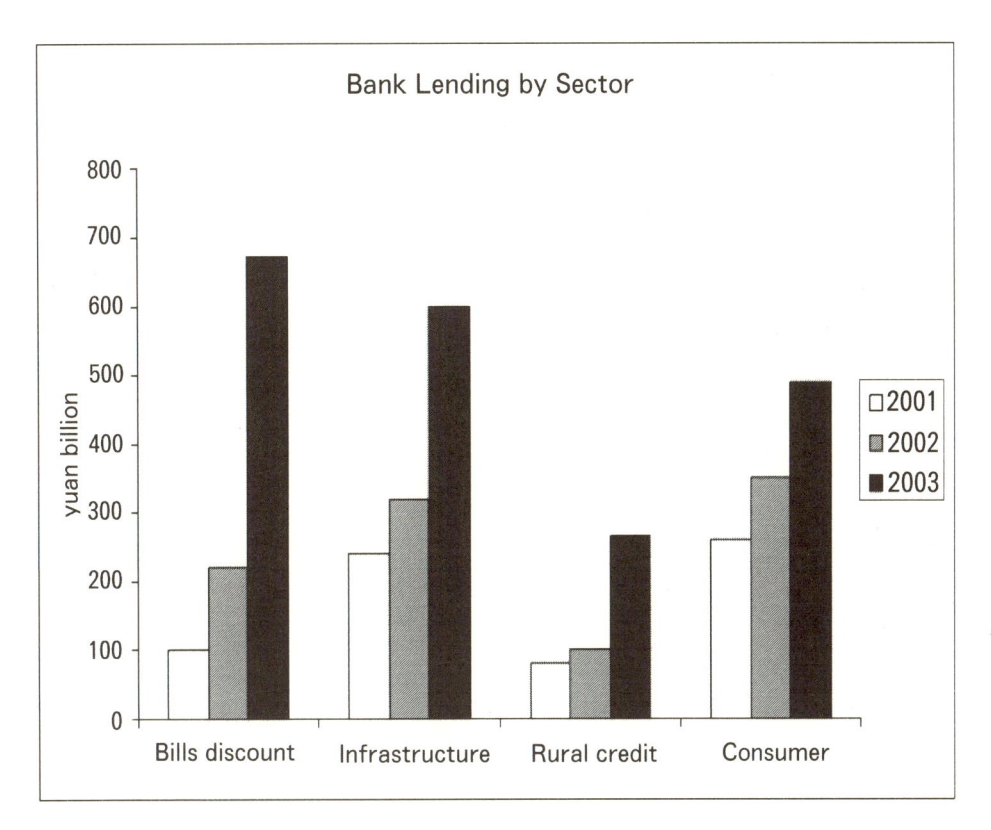

(Bar chart showing yuan billion for 2001, 2002, 2003 across Bills discount, Infrastructure, Rural credit, and Consumer sectors.)

Source: Zheng 2003a, p.12.

Figure 5-5

rate, although they can now make that view contingent on current conditions and adapt it to new information (this being the essence of what is meant by greater flexibility).

(3) Anchoring Monetary Policy

While much of this paper, like the surrounding debate, is framed in terms of choice of the exchange rate regime, the real question is the underlying objectives of monetary policy. Once upon a time, when normal instruments of monetary management were unavailable and exports were the only dynamic sector, it made sense to organize monetary policy around the currency peg. Exports determined economic growth and were strongly affected by the exchange rate. At the end of China's period of high inflation, the exchange rate was also the logical anchor for the price level. But these conditions no longer hold. Exports are no longer the exclusive driver of growth; the sources of demand for Chinese production have become more diversified. Price stability is well established, and an exchange rate peg is no longer the obvious focal point for monetary policy. As the capital account has grown more porous, capital displays a greater tendency to flow into the country when domestic and foreign interest rates diverse, limiting the authorities' room for maneuver. And as the economy is liberalized, creating new channels through which foreign capital can flow into the property market and other segments of the economy, the authorities' attempts to regulate money and credit conditions by issuing directives to the Big Four commercial banks becomes increasingly ineffectual. All this suggests that China needs to move to a more conventional monetary regime where interest rates are tailored to domestic conditions and where they can diverge from world 23 interest rates because the exchange rate is allowed to move. That the country possesses an inter-bank market and a central bank that engages in open market operations suggests that it is possible to regularize monetary policy in this way. Some will object that China lacks market-determined interest rates - that lending and deposit rates are still set by the central bank.

However, on January 1st, 2004, banks gained greater flexibility in terms of setting rates at variance with the central bank's pegs. Even if rates on some loans are still limited by official ceilings, it is rates on market-determined loans to private-owned firms and other customers that matter on the margin. And to the extent that increasing amounts of credit in any case circumvent the banking system completely, the absence of market-determined bank lending and deposit rates becomes less of an issue; those credit flows can only be shaped by adjusting interest rates. Another way of putting the point is that the authorities are going to have abandon their practice of setting bank lending and deposit rates at non-market levels sooner rather than later. To say that the PBOC should focus on growth and inflation does not mean that it can neglect exchange rate movements. How much weight it should put on the exchange rate in its reaction function and how widely the currency should be allowed to fluctuate should depend, in standard open-economy fashion, on the responsiveness of growth and inflation to shocks and the nature and magnitude of the specific shocks to which the economy is exposed. To repeat, the PBOC should think of itself as maximizing an objective function whose arguments are deviations from the target rate of inflation and the sustainable rate of growth. To many, this regime will sound like an informal version of open-economy inflation targeting, which of course is what it is. I am not arguing that China should immediately adopt the full apparatus of formal inflation targeting complete with issuance of an inflation report and a transparent policy making process. It is unlikely that Chinese officials would welcome the 24 requisite levels of transparency. But it is not clear that the entire formal apparatus is required to make this regime a success. In fact, countries like Peru which have adopted the relevant objective function and monetary policy operating strategy without also installing the complete apparatus have shown that this informal approach to inflation targeting can work. The PBOC already forecasts inflation and growth. China does not suffer from a problem of fiscal dominance like that which has prevented the operation of such regimes in other times and places.[35]

How much the exchange rate moves in this new regime will depend on the nature of shocks. Since these vary over time, it makes no sense to frame policy in terms of a time invariant fluctuation band. Thus, I do not see widening the width of the current fluctuation band as an effective way for the Chinese authorities to enhance their monetary control. If the band is widened slightly, say from plus-or-minus 0.3 per cent to plus-or-minus 3 per cent, there will remain the potential for conflict between the immediate goal of limiting exchange rate flexibility and the deeper objectives of achieving low inflation and sustainable growth. It then may be necessary to again shift the central parity, with all the difficulties and undesirable properties of a step revaluation. If the band is widened significantly more than this, then it will no longer serve as a guide for monetary policy. It is then best done away with.

To repeat, shunning a band need not mean that the exchange rate will fluctuate wildly.

The rate should be managed to limit the currency's movement. But the extent of permissible fluctuations should be a function of the shocks to which the economy is subjected, not of the width of a predetermined fluctuation band.

(4) Implications for Other Asian Countries

Assessing the impact of a change in the renminbi exchange rate on the rest of Asia is no easy task. Not only is there disagreement about how China itself will be affected, but there is confusion about how the impact will be felt by the country's neighbors.

On the assumption that China will continue to experience inflationary pressure, the PBOC will want to tighten monetary policy, which will imply some strengthening of the exchange rate going forward. The result will be to slightly slow the rate of economic growth relative to what would have obtained otherwise. As argued above, the large imported-input component of Chinese exports suggests that the impact on exports will be less than would be the case in a number of other countries. Similarly, the declining dependence of Chinese exports on the low cost of unskilled labor suggests that the impact will be smaller than might have been the case in earlier years.

This change in relative prices will lead to a reallocation of resources from the production of traded to non-traded goods (relative to the benchmark in which the exchange rate remains unchanged). Together with the elasticity of export growth with respect to GDP growth, this suggests that the change in the rate of growth of exports will be larger than the change in the rate of growth of the production of goods and services. (Historically, the change in the export growth rate relative to the change in the GDP growth rate is on the order to 2 to 3.) As export growth and GDP growth slow down at least slightly, so will the volume of inward FDI.

The rise in relative unit labor costs will accelerate the country's move out of unskilled labor intensive exports into products where labor costs matter less. It will speed the shift from the production of light manufactures (apparel, for example) into the production of finished capital goods such as data processing and office equipment, telecommunications equipment, and electrical machinery.

This implies that the impact on the country's Asian neighbors will be uneven. On the one hand, low-income countries such as Cambodia, Vietnam, Bangladesh, Sri Lanka, and Pakistan that compete with China in the production of unskilled-labor intensive light manufactures will benefit from the increase in China's relative unit labor costs and the country's shift into more technologically advanced, higher value-added product lines. These are the countries whose exports, broken down by industry, have the highest rank correlation with Chinese exports.[36] The same may be true of India, though less so insofar as the two countries specialize in different products (in apparel, for example, India specializes in undergarments while China specializes in outer garments). That China has as many as 200 million underemployed workers in agriculture and state enterprises yet to be absorbed into the modern sector, a significant fraction of whom will find work in export industries, suggests that the impact will not be great. Still, this logic suggests that the least developed Asian countries will benefit, ceteris paribus. The next tier of Asian countries will also feel the repercussions of higher Chinese labor costs, modestly relieving the pressure felt by their light manufacturing. But they will be less favorably affected insofar as the change in Chinese exchange rate policy will accelerate that country's move up the technology ladder into the product of more sophisticated goods. Here I have in mind countries like Thailand with which China increasingly competes in the production of higher valued-added products like household appliances and electrical machinery. Malaysia is plausibly in this group insofar as it competes with China both in light manufactures like non-textile clothing, furniture and textile yarn and in capital goods (automatic data processing machinery, electrical machinery, semiconductors, telecom parts and equipment, radio receivers and transistors) but has yet to move up the technology ladder to the same extent as Japan and the NIEs.[37] For present purposes we can assume that the positive impact on unskilled labor intensive industries and the negative impact on more skilled labor intensive industries roughly cancel out. The region's most advanced economies will feel mainly negative effects. Someday China will compete with them in the production of technologically-sophisticated inputs and capital goods. But that evolution will not be noticeably accelerated by the limited change in China's exchange rate contemplated here. This means that they will feel essentially no impact of the induced increase in

Chinese labor costs. The main way they will feel the change in exchange rate policy is as a deceleration in Chinese growth (relative to what would have happened otherwise) which will reduce the demand for their exports of capital goods.[38] Here I have in mind exports from Japan, Singapore, South Korea and Taiwan of parts and components for the assembly of consumer electronics and IT hardware (but also high quality textiles, machinery, equipment, and petrochemicals used in the production of other manufactures).[39] In the first nine months of 2003, China accounted for 36 per cent of total export growth in the case of South Korea, 32 per cent in the case of Japan, and 68 per cent in the case of Taiwan.[40] This is one basis for forecasting how these countries will feel the change in the rate of growth of Chinese manufacturing and exports.

This picture can of course be made more complicated by those with a taste for detail. For example, some of Asia's less developed countries export not only light manufactures to third markets but also energy products and agricultural staples to China; they will therefore feel some negative effects from the deceleration in Chinese growth.[41] Still, the basic story implies an improvement in international competitiveness for Asia's low income countries, a negligible net impact on the middle tier, and a negative impact on the upper tier. Note that the implications of this analysis of regional repercussions are very different than suggested in prior discussions. For example, contrary to the presumption of Bergsten (2004), it is not clear that a stronger renminbi will cause the dollar to depreciate against the currencies of the other advanced Asian economies (Japan, South Korea, Singapore, and Taiwan).[42] In addition, there is unlikely to be much impact on the currencies of middle-income Asian countries whose exports to the United States are also growing rapidly. This has obvious implications for the debate over global adjustment. A further argument, often heard, for allowing the RMB to adjust upward is that China, in formulating its exchange rate policy, should consider not just its own internal needs but also the global implications. As an increasingly large player on global markets, the country should be aware of its responsibility for the constructive correction of global imbalances. Conventional wisdom on this topic holds: first, that Asian currencies need to appreciate against the dollar in order to help correct the U.S. current account deficit without placing intolerable pressure on the European economy; and, second, that with appreciation of the RMB against the dollar, other Asian countries will be willing to allow their currencies to appreciate against the dollar as well. In fact, the analysis here suggests that appreciation of the renminbi will not put upward pressure on the yen, won and new Taiwan dollar. Whether the net effect of a stronger renminbi, including these additional repercussions, would be positive or negative for the U.S. current account deficit is uncertain. In my view, the main argument for a change in Chinese exchange rate policy stems from China's own domestic needs, not from any responsibility the country might have in helping to solve America's current account problem. For the United States, the solution to that problem lies at home.

The magnitude of the effects on the rest of Asia should not be exaggerated. Given the high imported-input content of Chinese exports of consumer electronics and IT hardware (as high as 84 per cent by some estimates), it is unlikely that the rate of growth of Chinese exports will slow dramatically even in the wake of a large devaluation. Hence there is unlikely to be a large impact on the country's neighbors. But what is critical to my discussion is not the magnitude but the direction of the effects - since previous analyses have suggested that an RMB revaluation will lead to a generalized revaluation of Asian currencies.

Four sources of evidence are consistent with my conclusions. First, there are simulation analyzes of the impact of China's emergence on the trade and growth of other countries, which generally take China's accession to the WTO as the comparative-statics experiment under consideration. To a first approximation, the effects of China's accession to the WTO increases its export market access -- and the access of other suppliers to China's home market - thus operating like a revaluation in reverse. Thus, Ianchovichina and Walmsley (2001) find that China's WTO access reduces the exports and therefore the GDP of Vietnam, the Philippines, Thailand and Indonesia and Malaysia (due mainly to the negative impact on their textile and apparel exports). A revaluation, which would raise Chinese labor costs and reduce the country's competitiveness in these sectors, would have precisely the opposite effects. They find that WTO accession would have a positive impact on exports of Japan and the NIEs (Hong Kong, South Korea, Singapore and Taiwan), due mainly to the increase in their exports to China of high quality textile and electronics inputs (along with miscellaneous exports of processing industries). Again this suggests that an RMB revaluation would have a negative impact on these countries. On the other hand, their simulations suggest a decline in exports (mainly of textiles and apparel) and a reduction in GDP relative to baseline levels in East Asia's developing countries. Similarly, Yang and Vines (2000) simulate the impact of China's growth on exports from other developing countries, finding that those of the ASEAN countries dropped slightly while those of Japan and the NIEs both rose.[43] Again, note that a stronger RMB that translates into somewhat slower Chinese growth in general and Chinese export growth in particular is tantamount to running this experiment in reverse. Second, there is the econometric study of Ahearne et al. (2003), which uses a panel of annual data spanning the period 1981-2000 for four NIEs (Korea, Singapore, Taiwan, and Hong Kong) and four ASEAN members (Indonesia, Malaysia, Philippines and Thailand).[44] The authors find (p.21) "little evidence that increases in China's exports reduce the exports of other emerging Asian economies. Indeed, it appears that China's exports and exports of the other countries are *positively* correlated" [emphasis in original]. This is exactly what my argument suggests should be the case for the four NIEs. Since these countries export components for use in China's own export industries, their exports will rise and - as in the case of revaluation - fall with the exports of the latter. Since Ahearne et al.'s four ASEAN members are in the middle tier of Asian countries, one should not be surprised by either a small positive or small negative coefficient on Chinese exports in their case.[45] My hypothesis suggests that one would find a negative coefficient when estimating the same equation for low-income Asian countries such as Cambodia, Vietnam, Bangladesh, Sri Lanka, and Pakistan. I do not yet know whether this is the case. But note that this is not the sample for which my results would be regarded as controversial. Rather, it is the positive correlation between China's exports and the export performance of high-income Asian countries that the advocates of yen revaluation to achieve global adjustment and U.S. current account rebalancing would regard as so controversial.

Third, there are the simulations that Warwick McKibbin has been kind enough to run using the G-Cubed model, of the effects a 10 per cent appreciation of the RMB (McKibbin and Stoeckel 2003). The G-Cubed Model is a dynamic macroeconomic model with considerable real and financial-sector disaggregation. Critically for present purposes, it distinguishes 12 Asian countries (counting Australia and New Zealand) and disaggregates by sector. These simulations show depreciations in the dollar exchange rates of essentially every Asian country within two years of China's revaluation against the dollar.

Fourth and finally, there is press commentary. Consider for example the headline and sub-head of story in the January 12, 2004 edition of the *Financial Times*: "China's growth helping to soak up excess Japanese capacity: Economists say strong demand from China may be weakening deflationary momentum in Japan."[46] Two further issues are worth noting in this context. The first one is Hong Kong. Essentially, Hong Kong is in the same situation as East Asia's other high-income countries, exporting high-quality textiles and other inputs utilized in Chinese manufacturing. Like Japan, South Korea, Singapore and Taiwan, it will suffer from the slowdown in Chinese growth and declining demand for its exports of intermediate goods. In addition, insofar as Hong Kong remains an important entrepot center, any deceleration of Chinese export growth will have an especially pronounced negative impact. On the other hand, there is the fact that Hong Kong stands to benefit disproportionately from the increase in Chinese tourism due to the increased purchasing power of the RMB. The net effect is uncertain. Then there are the implications for Hong Kong's currency board. Hong Kong's dollar peg has been especially convenient because the renminbi has also been tied to the dollar. When the RMB begins to float, the authorities will undoubted revisit this policy. An economy as small and open as Hong Kong has no wish to float. Pegging to the dollar has proven value but will grow less appealing as Hong Kong becomes even more economically interdependent with the Pearl River Delta and less interdependent with the United States. Shifting to a renminbi peg (or adopting the renminbi) is inevitable in the very long run. Yet, in the short run, abandoning the dollar peg would be a considerable shock to confidence. A possible compromise for the medium term would be to contemplate a basket peg with equal weights on the dollar and RMB. This brings us to the final issue, namely, proposals for a common basket or single currency peg for Asian countries. The fact that the competitiveness and exchange rates of different Asian countries will be affected in different ways also casts doubt on the notion that the region should respond with some kind of collective exchange rate arrangement. A common peg is not obviously desirable for a group of countries that will be affected in opposite directions by this common shock. A single currency peg for East Asia ex Japan, whether to the yen or the dollar, makes no sense when some countries will see their competitiveness enhanced by the change in Chinese exchange rate policy while others will see their competitiveness decline. A basket peg makes no more sense, insofar as different countries, which are affected in opposite directions, all peg to the same basket. Nor is it clear in which direction a basket with, say, equal weights on the yen, dollar and euro will move. Insofar as capital goods industries in the United States and Europe depend less than Japan's on exports of equipment to China, the deceleration in Chinese growth might lead to some strengthening of the dollar and euro against the yen. Yet even the direction, much less the magnitude, of the resulting change in an equally-weighted basket is impossible to predict.[47] From this point of view, it makes no sense to attempt to manage Asian exchange rates in the wake of the change in Chinese policy to prevent intra-regional fluctuations. Better than tying monetary policy to the dollar, the yen, a G-3 basket, or one another's currencies would be for the monetary authorities of each Asian country to focus on inflation and the output gap and to adjust interest rates and intervene in the foreign exchange market to target desirable levels for these variables.

(1) G. Hardin. J. Hered. 50, 68 (1959); S. von Hoernor, *Science* 137, 18 (1962).

(2) J. von Neumann and O. Morgenstern, *Theory of Games and Economic Behavior* (Princeton Univ. Press, Princeton, N.J., 1947), p. 11.

(3) J. H. Fremlin. *New Sci.*, No. 415 (1964), p. 285.

(4) A. Smith, *The Wealth of Nations* (Modern Library, New York, 1937), p. 423.

(5) W. F. Lloyd, *Two Lectures on the Checks to Population* (Oxford Univ. Press, Oxford, England, 1833), reprinted (in part) in *Population. Evolution, and Birth Control*, G. Hardin. Ed. (Freeman, San Francisco, 1964), p. 37.

(6) A. N. Whitehead, *Science and the Modern World* (Mentor, New York. 1948), p. 17.

(7) G. Hardin, Ed. *Population. Evolution. and Birth Control* (Freeman, San Francisco, 1964). p. 56.

(8) S. McVay, *Sci. Amer.* 216 (No. 8), 13 (1966).

(9) J. Fletcher, *Situation Ethics* (Westminster, Philadelphia, 1966).

(10) D. Lack, *The Natural Regulation of Animal Numbers* (Clarendon Press, Oxford, 1954).

(11) H. Girvetz, *From Wealth to Welfare* (Stanford Univ. Press. Stanford, Calif., 1950).

(12) G. Hardin, *Perspec. Biol. Med.* 6, 366 (1963).

(13) U. Thant. *Int. Planned Parenthood News,* No.168 (February 1968). p. 3.

(14) K. Davis, *Science* 158, 730 (1967).

(15) S. Tax, Ed., *Evolution after Darwin* (Univ. of Chicago Press, Chicago, 1960), vol. 2, p. 469.

(16) G. Bateson, D. D. Jackson, S. Haley, J. Weakland, *Behav. Sci.* 1. 251 (1956).

(17) P. Goodman, *New York Rev. Books* 10(8), 22 (23 May 1968).

(18) A. Comfort, *The Anxiety Makers* (Nebon, London, 1967).

(19) C. Frankel, *The Case for Modern Man* (Harper. New York, 1955), p. 203.

(20) J. D. Roslansky. *Genetics and the Future of Man* (Appleton-Century-Crofts, New York. 1966). p. 177.

(21) ASEAN 10 is a typical kind of South-to-South cooperation, which is highlighted by AFTA.

(22) It results from the multinationals' global production network the cross-nation production increases the trade of intermediate parts between China and ASEAN.

(23) The former was the so-called internal settlement rate of RMB2.8, which applied to all trade transactions. The official rate at the time was RMB1.5. The official rate, which gradually depreciated after the introduction of the internal settlement rate, continued to be used for non-trade transactions. The internal settlement rate was abolished at the end of 1984 when the official rate reached RMB2.8.

(24) However, interest rates on loans to small and medium size enterprises and rural credit cooperatives remain subject to administrative guidelines.

(25) A comprehensive survey is Cote (1994). This is in contrast to the results of studies of currency unification (e.g. Rose 2000), which detect larger effects from what is a monetary experiment of an entirely different kind.

(26) A change in the level of the exchange rate is another matter, but given the importance of imported inputs and components in their production, even the impact of this is likely to be limited. Jorian (1990) studied U.S. multinationals and found that their returns are significantly affected by exchange rate fluctuations in only one in ten cases. A more recent study by Ihring and Prior (2003) updates the data and disaggregates the data but succeeds in raising this fraction of firms to only 17-23 per cent.

(27) The aforementioned exports of foreign-investment enterprises and exports of state-owned enterprises together account for the rest.

(28) The rapid rise in money supply and bank credit in 2003 and 2004 was fueled not merely by the productivity and growth shocks that are the subject of this paragraph but also by anticipations of RMB revaluation (making for a less clean comparison than the data for 2002).

(29) If the Chinese authorities were prepared to tighten capital controls, the story would then be different. But such a policy would run counter to their stated intentions and recent actions (as noted above), not to mention with trends in the vast majority of other countries.

(30) That said, the state sector as a result of restructuring has shed some 50 million jobs (and continues to do so at the rate of 7-9 million jobs per annum). This suggests that a currency adjustment that results in the loss of 1 million jobs will not be an unmanageable political burden.

(31) Diversification implying greater stability insofar as monetary policies in different countries are imperfectly correlated with one another.

(32) References by, inter alia, Taylor (2003) to a flexible or "market determined" exchange rate regime (which presumably means an exchange rate not influenced by official intervention, as opposed to a managed float)

(33) Others, like Merrill Lynch (2004, p.3), reach the same conclusion (e.g. "The 'closed' capital account is clearly showing signs of leakage...Intervention required to offset these flows is simply too large to easily sterilize and, as a result, the external imbalance is generating internal discord").

(34) Studies of other regulated capital account regimes, such as Chile's, generally suggest that their restrictions on capital account transactions have tended to lose effectiveness over time.

(35) To be sure, the weakness of the state enterprises and, especially, the banking system mean that the likelihood of such problems down the road should not be minimized. If those problems are put off until they finally explode, with serious adverse consequences for public-sector finances, the PBOC's commitment to low inflation could be placed at risk. But so too would be any other monetary policy regime, including one predicated on the continued maintenance of a currency peg. These problems are not arguments against a more flexible exchange rate per se. But they are an argument for resolving problems in the state-enterprise and banking sectors as quickly as possible so that the pursuit of a stable monetary policy, whatever the regime, is not placed at risk.

(36) See Shafaeddin (2002). One should be careful here, because these rank correlations are based on historical data and the structure of exports is changing rapidly.

(37) Some might also put Indonesia and the Philippines in this category.

(38) As Kanno (2003, p.14) writes, "[if] f China's capex-driven growth were to slow, Japan would suffer" (Kanno 2003, p.14). 10 per cent of Japanese exports went to China in 2002, up from 5 per cent in 1995. China accounted for 39 per cent of Japan's export growth in 2002 and 32 per cent in 2003.

(39) Textiles are a good example. Japan, Hong Kong, Taiwan and Korea export high quality textiles to China as inputs into its exports of clothing. They benefit from low labor costs there, while lower income countries suffer (Ianchovichina, Suthiwart-Narueput and Zhao 2003).

(40) Preliminary data. In the ASEAN countries, in contrast, the China share was 20-30 per cent. This reinforces the preceding point about how ASEAN ex Singapore on the one hand and Japan, South Korea and Taiwan on the other will feel quite different effects.

(41) This is likely to be especially true of Indonesia, whose exports are relatively natural resource intensive (the country exports energy, timber, oilseeds, sugar and cotton to China). Thailand and Vietnam will also be hurt by slower Chinese growth insofar as they export cereals to that country.

(42) "Korea, other Asian countries and even Japan are understandably reluctant to let their currencies rise against the dollar when doing so would produce an equivalent rise against the renminbi,

the money of their toughest competitor" (Bergsten 2004, p.3). This no longer follows if the exports of China and these countries are complements, not substitutes.

(43) These overall effects are the sum of positive effects on exports to China itself and negative effects on exports to third markets, which differ in size depending on the Asian exporter concerned - as emphasized in my discussion above.

(44) Singapore is also a member of ASEAN. Here I am simply following Ahearne et al's categorization.

(45) Note that these effects are only statistically significant when the authors do not control for common shocks.

(46) Kynge and Pilling (2004), p.10. Or see the *FT* article on 27 January 2004, "Surge in Japanese Exports to China," describing how growing Japanese exports of components to the Chinese economy has been supporting the yen.

(47) Recently, especially in the developing country, it tends to be selected either severe Fixed Exchange Rate System such as the currency boards and dollarizations or the Floating Exchange Rate System. However, the intermediate system might be actually preferable. For instance, it is "BBC rule" (Basket, Band, Crawling) etc. on which John Williamson is insisting.

Chapter 6　The regional cooperation in Europe

Section 1　The reason to stick together for the future

For centuries, Europe was the scene of frequent and bloody wars. In the period 1870 to 1945, France and Germany fought each other three times, with terrible loss of life. A number of European leaders became convinced that the only way to secure a lasting peace between their countries was to unite them economically and politically.

So, in 1950, in a speech inspired by Jean Monnet, the French Foreign Minister Robert Schuman proposed integrating the coal and steel industries of Western Europe. A result, in 1951, the European Coal and Steel Community (ECSC) was set up, with six members: Belgium, West Germany, Luxembourg, France, Italy and the Netherlands. The power to take decisions about the coal and steel industry in these countries was placed in the hands of an independent, supranational body called the "High Authority". Jean Monnet was its first President.

The ECSC was such a success that, within a few years, these same six countries decided to go further and integrate other sectors of their economies. In 1957 they signed the Treaties of Rome, creating the European Atomic Energy Community (EURATOM) and the European Economic Community (EEC). The member states set about removing trade barriers between them and forming a "common market".

In 1967 the institutions of the three European communities were merged. From this point on, there was a single Commission and a single Council of Ministers as well as the European Parliament.

Originally, the members of the European Parliament were chosen by the national parliaments but in 1979 the first direct elections were held, allowing the citizens of the member states to vote for the candidate of their choice. Since then, direct elections have been held every five years.

The Treaty of Maastricht (1992) introduced new forms of co-operation between the member state governments - for example on defense, and in the area of "justice and home affairs". By adding this inter-governmental co-operation to the existing "Community" system, the Maastricht Treaty created the European Union (EU).

Economic and political integration between the member states of the European Union means that these countries have to take joint decisions on many matters. So they have developed common policies in a very wide range of fields - from agriculture to culture, from consumer affairs to competition, from the environment and energy to transport and trade. In the early days the focus was on a common commercial policy for coal and steel and a common agricultural policy. Other policies were added as time went by, and as the need arose. Some key policy aims have changed in the light of changing circumstances. For example, the aim of the agricultural policy is no longer to produce as much food as cheaply as possible but to support farming methods that produce healthy, high-quality food and protect the environment. The need for environmental protection is now taken into account across the whole range of EU policies.

The European Union's relations with the rest of the world have also become important. The EU negotiates major trade and aid agreements with other countries and is developing a Common Foreign and Security Policy.

It took some time for the Member States to remove all the barriers to trade between them and to turn their "common market" into a genuine single market in which goods, services, people and capital could move around freely. The Single Market was formally completed at the end of 1992, though there is still work to be done in some areas - for example, to create a genuinely single market in financial services.

During the 1990s it became increasingly easy for people to move around in Europe, as passport and customs checks were abolished at most of the EU's internal borders. One consequence is greater mobility for EU citizens. Since 1987, for example, more than a million young Europeans have taken study courses abroad, with support from the EU.

In 1992 the EU decided to go for economic and monetary union (EMU), involving the introduction of a single European currency managed by a European Central Bank. The single currency - the euro - became a reality on 1 January 2002, when euro notes and coins replaced national currencies in twelve of the 15 countries of the European Union (Belgium, Germany, Greece, Spain, France, Ireland, Italy, Luxembourg, the Netherlands, Austria, Portugal and Finland).

The EU has grown in size with successive waves of accessions. Denmark, Ireland and the United Kingdom joined in 1973 followed by Greece in 1981, Spain and Portugal in 1986 and Austria, Finland and Sweden in 1995. The European Union welcomed ten new countries in 2004: Cyprus, the Czech Republic, Estonia, Hungary, Latvia, Lithuania, Malta, Poland, Slovakia and Slovenia. Bulgaria and Romania expect to follow in 2007; Croatia and Turkey are beginning membership negotiations in 2005.To ensure that the enlarged EU can continue functioning efficiently, it needs a more streamlined system for taking decisions. That is why the Treaty of Nice lays down new rules governing the size of the EU institutions and the way they work. It came into force on 1 February 2003. It will be replaced, in 2006, by the new EU Constitution - if all EU countries approve this.

Section 2　The practical system of European monetary system

(1) The European Monetary System

Instituted in 1979, the EMS established an adjustable peg exchange rate system between most European Community member states and a floating rate with countries outside the system. The EMS agreement contained explicit rules governing exchange rates, intervention in exchange markets, and currency realignments. Each member state agreed to maintain the market exchange rate of its currency within fixed margins above or below a bilateral central rate(1), usually within 2.25 percent around the official rate(2).

The rules for currency realignments required that countries requesting a realignment appeal to the Monetary Committee, composed of officials from member state finance ministries and central banks, to negotiate the size and timing of the adjustment. In practice, the Committee always limited the size of a devaluation, making it smaller than the proposal made by the devaluing government. Additionally, the upper bound of the new parity always fell within the boundaries of the old parity, as a deterrent to speculators (DeGrauwe 1992). Finally, the Monetary Committee sometimes placed pressure on the devaluing government to tighten its economic policies to lend credibility to the new parity.

Despite the ability for national governments to pursue divergent monetary policies within the EMS, the EMS experience was marked by a gradual convergence of monetary policy outcomes across member states. In each member state, inflation fell throughout the early 1980s and remained relatively stable in the latter half of the decade. Germany was the system's low inflation leader throughout most of the decade. Since German monetary unification in 1990, however, other EMS countries, including France, have outperformed Germany.

As a result of this macroeconomic convergence, the frequency of currency realignments within the EMS decreased (Gros and Thygesen 1992). During the first four years of operation (1979-1983), seven currency realignments occurred, culminating with a general realignment in March 1983. By the end of the period, the French franc had lost over 30 percent of its value against the D-mark. The next four years saw only four devaluations. And, unlike earlier realignments, speculative unrest in currency markets, rather than macroeconomic divergence, precipitated the final realignment in January 1987. From 1987 until the crash of the EMS in September 1992, no devaluations occurred.

(2) The EMS as a Coordinating Device

I argue that the exchange rate stability within EMS emerged as a focal point for domestic publics. Compliance with exchange rate stability had predictable macroeconomic consequences that complemented the policy goals of social coalitions in favor of macroeconomic discipline-that is, greater fiscal responsibility and price stability. And, since the EMS provided an easily observable standard, this social coalition could punish governments that violated exchange rate stability, changing the government's political incentives over monetary policy and exchange rate cooperation.[3] This section considers the economic consequences of fixed exchange rates in the EMS, the preferences of different sectors, and the monitor ability of exchange rate movements in the EMS to explain why exchange rate stability emerged as a focal point.

Adherence to a fixed exchange rate implies a loss of monetary policy autonomy. According to the Mundell-Fleming model, countries can attain only two of the three following conditions: capital mobility, fixed exchange rates, or national policy autonomy. During the 1980s, both technological advances and regulatory liberalization of the financial sector throughout Europe dramatically increased the volume of international capital movement (Goodman and Pauly 1993; Sandholtz 1993). In a world of capital mobility, real interest rates must be the same across borders. EMS member governments, therefore, had to mimic the economic policies of the most disciplined country to maintain a fixed exchange rate, losing the ability to manipulate policy for domestic policy objectives. In practical terms, member states had to match the Germany's monetary discipline if they wished to maintain the exchange rate.

As a result of the differential rates of inflation across EMS member states, the commitment to fixed (nominal) exchange rates implied a relatively appreciated (real) exchange rate against the D-mark. This appreciation reduced aggregate demand generally, dampened economic growth, and worsened the current account balance. The appreciation also affected the relative prices of tradable and non-tradable goods within each member state, raising the domestic prices of non-tradable goods and services relative to the domestic price of tradables.

Devaluation offers relief from the macroeconomic pressures brought on by this real appreciation. By making exports cheaper and increasing demand for domestically produced import substitutes, devaluation can produce temporary improvements in employment and the current account (Cukierman 1992; Krugman and Obstfeld 1991). In the long-term, however, devaluation does not alter demand or supply conditions, instead producing only a proportional increase in the price level. Devaluation, therefore, indicates the government's economic policies were more expansionary than the country's key trading partners.

These macroeconomic and distributional consequences shape the preferences of various economic sectors over a fixed exchange rate commitment (Frieden 1994; 1991). International traders and investors as well as export producers who compete on non-price dimensions value the stability of the exchange rate over domestic policy autonomy. Commitment to a fixed exchange rate implies greater predictability in foreign trade and exchange, reducing the riskiness of their transactions. Devaluations, however, introduce uncertainty about the exchange rate. In contrast, producers of tradable goods that compete primarily on price-either exporters or import competitors-favor a flexible exchange rate and a weak currency. Devaluation helps them compete with imports or in export markets.

Producers of non-tradable goods have more ambivalent preferences over the commitment to a fixed exchange rate. Although the relative price effects of a relatively appreciated currency benefit them, nontaxable place more emphasis on pursuing domestic policy objectives rather than maintaining a fixed exchange rate. Exchange rate volatility has few direct consequences for them. Instead, their domestic macroeconomic goals determine their stance toward the exchange rate commitment. If non-tradables desire policies, which differ from potential partners in an exchange rate regime, then they will oppose a fixed exchange rate. But if non-tradables have policy goals, which are similar to those potential partners, they may look to a fixed exchange rate commitment as a way to insure that their government achieves those goals. In the EMS, a commitment to a fixed exchange rate with Germany implied more disciplined monetary and fiscal policies domestically. Consequently, producers in the non-tradables sector who were exasperated with the high inflation of the late 1970s could consider the government's ability to maintain a fixed exchange rate as an indicator of the government's overall macroeconomic policy discipline.[4]

In the context of the EMS, devaluations and exchange rate stability provided an easily monitorable standard with which to evaluate the government's monetary policy decisions. Currency realignments were a media event. Newspapers and television covered the negotiations between the devaluing member state and the Monetary Committee. The discrete and sometimes dramatic nature of a devaluation focused attention on the government's economic policies (Alt 1991). Additionally, the media emphasis on devaluations meant that the public did not have to monitor the government's policy continuously. Instead, they could have confidence that the absence of a devaluation signaled that the government's macroeconomic policy was dedicated to the goals of price stability. Devaluation, on the other hand, sent a clear signal to the contrary.

Even in the absence of devaluation, however, the currency bands of the EMS provided a baseline with which to judge exchange rate movements. Newspapers and television throughout Europe regularly report exchange rates, often emphasizing the currency's standing against the D-mark. Sharp swings in the exchange rate or consistent trends in exchange rate movements toward one of the bands provided information about the government's policy choices. Without the currency bands around the bilateral rates within the EMS, the public lacked a common, observable standard with which to assess the movements in the exchange rate.

Exchange rate stability within the EMS, therefore, became a focal point for domestic publics. Maintenance of exchange rate stability had relatively predictable consequences for macroeconomic performance and it provided an observable standard to evaluate policy. Within EMS member states, domestic social coalitions in favor of macroeconomic discipline-internationally oriented actors, some exporters, and non-tradables-soon realized that exchange rate movements signaled their government's monetary policy stance, quickly equating their goals of fiscal responsibility and price stability with exchange rate stability. A devaluation raised questions about the government's commitment to macroeconomic discipline.

Devaluation also hurts the government's overall credibility. To prevent currency speculation, a government has to issue assurances that it would maintain the currency's parity. After a devaluation, however, the government must justify the decision to devalue with its earlier defense of the exchange rate bands. These policy "flip-flops" raise doubt about the government's trustworthiness.

Since these domestic social coalitions could monitor their government's policy choices and punish the government electorally if it violated the standard of exchange rate stability, member state governments had short-term political incentives to maintain their exchange rate parity, helping to maintain governments' policy discipline.

(3) Government Accountability in the EMS: An Empirical Examination

To test the relationship between devaluations in the EMS, economic outcomes, and government accountability, I examine the relationship between government approval ratings and monetary policy in France. Specifically, I test whether devaluations negatively affected the government's approval ratings.

The French case is important for several reasons. First, the French rejection of statistic economic management in favor of macroeconomic discipline is representative of a larger trend throughout Europe. Although most observers point to Mitterrand's sudden shift to economic "rigueur" as the turning point for French economic policy, Mitterrand's U-turn actually represented a continuation of major reforms initiated under his predecessors. By the mid-1980s, French policymakers had abolished their system of credit controls and established broader and deeper financial markets, culminating with the adoption of monetary policy mechanisms based on indirect instruments designed to influence interest rates.

Second, France plays a major role in the European Union. During the 1970s and 1980s, France provided other member states with an alternative to the German economic model. France's acceptance of macroeconomic discipline reinvigorated Europe's development, sparking the internal market program, clearing the way for the "hardening" of the EMS in the late 1980s, and shaping the groundwork for monetary union. It is important, therefore, to understand how European institutions interacted with French domestic politics to influence the Europe-wide policy consensus in support of macroeconomic discipline.

Section 3　The impact of EURO

(1) **European financial markets and the euro**
Government bond markets

　The spreads of euro area 10-year government bonds versus the German Bund have fallen since the birth of the euro and are now at very low levels. In February 2004, the Austrian bond was trading at 3 basis points above the Bund, the French bond 2 bp; the Finnish bond -2 bp; the Dutch bond 0 bp; the Italian bond at +14 bp. Since currency risk is now absent and since there are few reasons to believe that default risks have changed much over the past five years, this suggests that the liquidity risk on those markets has been falling. There is now as well some evidence that market participants have been coordinating on some key securities, which have become benchmark securities for the government bond market. These are the German Bund at 10 years, the French bond at 5 years and the Italian bond at 2 years. The existence of such benchmark securities facilitates the process of price discovery and the well-functioning of markets.

Corporate bond markets

　Corporate bond markets were almost inexistent for non-financial and non-monetary institutions in 1998. So were markets for 'junk' bonds. But corporate bond markets as a whole underwent a substantial development after the birth of the euro. Total corporate sector issuances amounted to less than □150 bn in 1998. It increased to □360 bn in 1999; □250 bn in 2000; □300 bn in 2001; □250 bn in 2002. It increased again in 2003.

Derivatives market

　The euro swap market was at the beginning of 2003 the largest financial market in the world with more than 25 trillion euros outstanding. Just as a matter of comparison, the total amount of dollar denominated money market instruments and bonds issued by governments and non-governments in domestic and international markets was just around 20 trillion euros at the same time.

Equity markets

　European equity markets have been traditionally quite segmented. The advent of the euro seems to have fostered a greater degree of financial integration. The degree of correlation between equity price indices in the major markets has kept on increasing (but it has been doing so ever since the beginning of the 1990s. More strikingly, the share of equities invested in Europe-wide funds has gone up substantially in euro area countries to become close to 50%. A similar increase has not been observed for the countries, which have chosen to remain outside the euro area (Denmark, UK, Switzerland).

Euro area financial markets have therefore become more liquid, more diverse and more integrated since the birth of the euro. On the international side however, the dollar has remained the key international currency, by most measures.

(2) International role of the euro

Foreign exchange trading in euros as a percent of global trade has not increased compared to the share of EMS currencies. In 1998, the dollar was present 87.3% of the time at one end of a transaction on the foreign exchange market while the EMS currencies were present 52.5% of the time (note that the percentages sum up to 200% since transactions involved pair of currencies). In 2001, the share of the dollar was 90.4% and the share of the euro was a mere 37.6%. All the intra-European trades have been netted out with the arrival of the euro so in fact that there is no dramatic fall in the share of the euro compared to EMS currency, but there is no increase either. Similarly although the share of the euro in reserves has been gradually increasing over time it only amounted to 18.7% in 2002 compared to 64.5% for the dollar.

The role of the euro for international trade in goods (invoicing currency) has also markedly increased but is still below the dollar level. For example in 2002 55.3% of French export of goods were invoiced in euros. The comparable number was only 48% in 2000. Similarly only 35% of French imports were invoiced in euro in 2000. In 2002 46.8% were. As regional integration has been proceeding further in Europe, the share of exports and imports invoiced and settled in euro has increased to approximately 60% to 80% for countries which will accede to the European Union (such as Bulgaria, Cyprus, Czech Republic, Hungary, Latvia, Poland, Romania, etc...)

But it is in the realm of international debt issuance that the euro has taken on more clearly its international role. The stock of international debt denominated in euros (excluding home country issuance) has risen from below 20% at then end of 1998 to just above 30% oat the beginning of 2003.

The euro has successfully completed its first five years of existence. It has triggered important changes in European financial markets. It has also established itself immediately as the second most important currency in the world and as a potential competitor to the US dollar. It has however not displaced in any significant way the dollar as the currency of choice for most international transactions and as a reserve currency. The main reason for this is the inherent inertia of the international monetary system (see Krugman 1980, Rey 2001). Once a currency is at the center of the system it is very difficult for other currencies to compete with the incumbent since no economic agents finds it desirable to use a currency different from the one that everybody else is using. It has taken a long time before pound sterling lost ground as an international currency and was replaced by the dollar, which had become a credible alternative over the years as the US grew to become the biggest economy in the world (and its biggest exporter and importer). The dramatic change between the sterling and the dollar occurred only after two world wars, after the stability of the sterling was significantly undermined, after the shrinkage of the importance of the UK in the world economy and after the establishment of Bretton Woods.

(1) Each currency within the exchange rate mechanism had a central rate, defined as the price of that currency in ECUs, a (weighted) basket of member state currencies. The ratio of central rates between two currencies served as the bilateral rate between currencies.

(2) Italy was an exception to this relatively tight exchange rate band. The lira was allowed to fluctuate at plus or minus 6 percent around the central rate. Newer entrants to the system, Spain (1989) and Britain (1990), were also permitted to fluctuate within the wider $+/-6$ percent band.

(3) In contrast, Woolley (1992) suggests that the electorate will punish their governments for devaluations since they view international commitments as more serious than domestic policy commitments.

(4) Frieden (1994) also recognizes that non-tradables were indifferent about France's commitment to the EMS. He argues that support for a fixed exchange rate was achieved by linking the issue of monetary integration to further European integration.

Chapter 7 Globalization and Governance

Section 1 The movement of Hegemony

(1) **The U.S. power**

The onset of international economic stagnation in the 1970s had two important consequences for U. S. power. First, stagnation resulted in the collapse of "developmentalism" economically if the state took appropriate action ideological claim of the Old Left movements then in power. One after another, these regimes faced internal disorder, declining standards of living, increasing debt dependency on international financial institutions, and eroding credibility. What had seemed in the 1960s to be the successful navigation of Third World decolonization by the United States disruption and maximizing the smooth transfer of power to regimes that were developmentalist but scarcely revolutionary order, simmering discontents, and unchanneled radical temperaments. When the United States tried to intervene, it failed. In 1983, U.S. President Ronald Reagan sent troops to Lebanon to restore order. The troops were in effect forced out. He compensated by invading Grenada, a country without troops. President George H.W. Bush invaded Panama, another country without troops. But after he intervened in Somalia to restore order, the United States was in effect forced out, somewhat ignominiously. Since there was little the U. S. government could actually do to reverse the trend of declining hegemony, it chose simply to ignore this trend the withdrawal from Vietnam until September 11, 2001.

Meanwhile, true conservatives began to assume control of key states and interstate institutions. The neo-liberal offensive of the 1980s was marked by the Thatcher and Reagan regimes and the emergence of the International Monetary Fund (IMF) as a key actor on the world scene. Where once (for more than a century) conservative forces had attempted to portray themselves as wiser liberals, now centrist liberals were compelled to argue that they were more effective conservatives. The conservative programs were clear. Domestically, conservatives tried to enact policies that would reduce the cost of labor, minimize environmental constraints on producers, and cut back on state welfare benefits. Actual successes were modest, so conservatives then moved vigorously into the international arena. The gatherings of the World Economic Forum in Davos provided a meeting ground for elites and the media. The IMF provided a club for finance ministers and central bankers. And the United States pushed for the creation of the World Trade Organization to enforce free commercial flows across the world's frontiers.

While the United States wasn't watching, the Soviet Union was collapsing. Yes, Ronald Reagan had dubbed the Soviet Union an "evil empire" and had used the rhetorical bombast of calling for the destruction of the Berlin Wall, but the United States didn't really mean it and certainly was not responsible for the Soviet Union's downfall. In truth, the Soviet Union and its East European imperial zone collapsed because of popular disillusionment with the Old Left in combination with Soviet leader Mikhail Gorbachev's efforts to save his regime by liquidating Yalta and instituting internal liberalization (perestroika plus glasnost). Gorbachev succeeded in liquidating Yalta but not in saving the Soviet Union (although he almost did, be it said).

The United States was stunned and puzzled by the sudden collapse, uncertain how to handle the consequences. The collapse of communism in effect signified the collapse of liberalism, removing the only ideological justification behind U.S. hegemony, a justification tacitly supported by liberalism's ostensible ideological opponent. This loss of legitimacy led directly to the Iraqi invasion of Kuwait, which Iraqi leader Saddam Hussein would never have dared had the Yalta arrangements remained in place. In retrospect, U.S. efforts in the Gulf War accomplished a truce at basically the same line of departure. But can a hegemonic power be satisfied with a tie in a war with a middling regional power? Saddam demonstrated that one could pick a fight with the United States and get away with it. Even more than the defeat in Vietnam, Saddam's brash challenge has eaten at the innards of the U.S. right, in particular those known as the hawks, which explains the fervor of their current desire to invade Iraq and destroy its regime.

Between the Gulf War and September 11, 2001, the two major arenas of world conflict were the Balkans and the Middle East. The United States has played a major diplomatic role in both regions. Looking back, how different would the results have been had the United States assumed a completely isolationist position? In the Balkans, an economically successful multinational state (Yugoslavia) broke down, essentially into its component parts. Over 10 years, most of the resulting states have engaged in a process of ethnification, experiencing fairly brutal violence, widespread human rights violations, and outright wars. Outside intervention United States figured most prominently most egregious violence, but this intervention in no way reversed the ethnification, which is now consolidated and somewhat legitimated. Would these conflicts have ended differently without U.S. involvement? The violence might have continued longer, but the basic results would probably not have been too different. The picture is even grimmer in the Middle East, where, if anything, U.S. engagement has been deeper and its failures more spectacular. In the Balkans and the Middle East alike, the United States has failed to exert its hegemonic clout effectively, not for want of will or effort but for want of real power.

(2) **After the September 11**

Then came September 11 legislators, the Central Intelligence Agency (CIA) now claims it had warned the Bush administration of possible threats. But despite the CIA's focus on al Qaeda and the agency's intelligence expertise, it could not foresee (and therefore, prevent) the execution of the terrorist strikes. Or so would argue CIA Director George Tenet. This testimony can hardly comfort the U.S. government or the American people. Whatever else historians may decide, the attacks of September 11, 2001, posed a major challenge to U.S. power. The persons responsible did not represent a major military power. They were members of a non-state force, with a high degree of determination, some money, a band of dedicated followers, and a strong base in one weak state. In short, militarily, they were nothing. Yet they succeeded in a bold attack on U.S. soil.

George W. Bush came to power very critical of the Clinton administration's handling of world affairs. Bush and his advisors did not admit undoubtedly aware president since Gerald Ford, including that of Ronald Reagan and George H.W. Bush. It had even been the path of the current Bush administration before September 11. One only needs to look at how Bush handled the downing of the U.S. plane off China in April 2001 to see that prudence had been the name of the game.

Following the terrorist attacks, Bush changed course, declaring war on terrorism, assuring the American people that "the outcome is certain" and informing the world that "you are either with us or against us." Long frustrated by even the most conservative U.S. administrations, the hawks finally came to dominate American policy. Their position is clear: The United States wields overwhelming military power, and even though countless foreign leaders consider it unwise for Washington to flex its military muscles, these same leaders cannot and will not do anything if the United States simply imposes its will on the rest. The hawks believe the United States should act as an imperial power for two reasons: First, the United States can get away with it. And second, if Washington doesn't exert its force, the United States will become increasingly marginalized.

Today, this hawkish position has three expressions: the military assault in Afghanistan, the de facto support for the Israeli attempt to liquidate the Palestinian Authority, and the invasion of Iraq, which is reportedly in the military preparation stage. Less than one year after the September 2001 terrorist attacks, it is perhaps too early to assess what such strategies will accomplish. Thus far, these schemes have led to the overthrow of the Taliban in Afghanistan (without the complete dismantling of al Qaeda or the capture of its top leadership); enormous destruction in Palestine (without rendering Palestinian leader Yasir

Arafat "irrelevant," as Israeli Prime Minister Ariel Sharon said he is); and heavy opposition from U.S. allies in Europe and the Middle East to plans for an invasion of Iraq.

The hawk's reading of recent events emphasizes that opposition to U.S. actions, while serious, has remained largely verbal. Neither Western Europe nor Russia nor China nor Saudi Arabia has seemed ready to break ties in serious ways with the United States. In other words, hawks believe, Washington has indeed gotten away with it. The hawks assume a similar outcome will occur when the U.S. military actually invades Iraq and after that, when the United States exercises its authority elsewhere in the world, be it in Iran, North Korea, Colombia, or perhaps Indonesia. Ironically, the hawk reading has largely become the reading of the international left, which has been screaming about U.S. policies chances of U.S. success are high.

But hawk interpretations are wrong and will only contribute to the United State's decline, transforming a gradual descent into a much more rapid and turbulent fall. Specifically, hawk approaches will fail for military, economic, and ideological reasons.

Undoubtedly, the military remains the United State's strongest card; in fact, it is the only card. Today, the United States wields the most formidable military apparatus in the world. And if claims of new, unmatched military technologies are to be believed, the U.S. military edge over the rest of the world is considerably greater today than it was just a decade ago. But does that mean, then, that the United States can invade Iraq, conquer it rapidly, and install a friendly and stable regime? Unlikely, Bear in mind that of the three serious wars the U.S. military has fought since 1945 (Korea, Vietnam, and the Gulf War), one ended in defeat and two in draws Saddam Hussein's army is not that of the Taliban, and his internal military control is far more coherent. A U.S. invasion would necessarily involve a serious land force, one that would have to fight its way to Baghdad and would likely suffer significant casualties. Such a force would also need staging grounds, and Saudi Arabia has made clear that it will not serve in this capacity. Would Kuwait or Turkey help out? Perhaps, if Washington calls in all its chips. Meanwhile, Saddam can be expected to deploy all weapons at his disposal, and it is precisely the U.S. government that keeps fretting over how nasty those weapons might be. The United States may twist the arms of regimes in the region, but popular sentiment clearly views the whole affair as reflecting a deep anti-Arab bias in the United States. Can such a conflict be won? The British General Staff has apparently already informed Prime Minister Tony Blair that it does not believe so.

And there is always the matter of "second fronts." Following the Gulf War, U.S. armed forces sought to prepare for the possibility of two simultaneous regional wars. After a while, the Pentagon quietly abandoned the idea as impractical and costly. But who can be sure that no potential U.S. enemies would strike when the United States appears bogged down in Iraq?

Consider, too, the question of U.S. popular tolerance of non-victories. Americans hover between a patriotic fervor that lends support to all wartime presidents and a deep isolationist urge. Since 1945, patriotism has hit a wall whenever the death toll has risen. Why should today1s reaction differ? And even if the hawks (who are almost all civilians) feel impervious to public opinion, U.S. Army generals, burnt by Vietnam, do not.

And what about the economic front? In the 1980s, countless American analysts became hysterical over the Japanese economic miracle. They calmed down in the 1990s, given Japan's well-publicized financial difficulties. Yet after overstating how quickly Japan was moving forward, U.S. authorities now seem to be complacent, confident that Japan lags far behind. These days, Washington seems more inclined to lecture Japanese policymakers about what they are doing wrong.

Such triumphalism hardly appears warranted. Consider the following April 20, 2002, New York Times report: A Japanese laboratory has built the world's fastest computer, a machine so powerful that it matches the raw processing power of the 20 fastest American computers combined and far outstrips the previous leader, an I.B.M.-built machine. The achievement... is evidence that a technology race that most American engineers thought they were winning handily is far from over. The analysis goes on to note that there are "contrasting scientific and technological priorities" in the two countries. The Japanese machine is built to analyze climatic change, but U.S. machines are designed to simulate weapons. This contrast embodies the oldest story in the history of hegemonic powers. The dominant power concentrates (to its detriment) on the military; the candidate for successor concentrates on the economy. The latter has always paid off, handsomely. It did for the United States. Why should it not pay off for Japan as well, perhaps in alliance with China?

Finally, there is the ideological sphere. Right now, the U.S. economy seems relatively weak, even more so considering the exorbitant military expenses associated with hawk strategies. Moreover, Washington remains politically isolated; virtually no one (save Israel) thinks the hawk position makes sense or is worth encouraging. Other nations are afraid or unwilling to stand up to Washington directly, but even their foot-dragging is hurting the United States.

Yet the U.S. response amounts to little more than arrogant arm-twisting. Arrogance has its own negatives. Calling in chips means leaving fewer chips for next time, and surly acquiescence breeds increasing resentment. Over the last 200 years, the United States acquired a considerable amount of ideological credit. But these days, the United States is running through this credit even faster than it ran through its gold surplus in the 1960s.

The United States faces two possibilities during the next 10 years: It can follow the hawk's path, with negative consequences for all but especially for itself. Or it can realize that the negatives are too great. Simon Tisdall of the Guardian recently argued that even disregarding international public opinion, the U.S. is not able to fight a successful Iraqi war by itself without incurring immense damage, not least in terms of its economic interests and its energy supply. Mr. Bush is reduced to talking tough and looking ineffectual. And if the United States still invades Iraq and is then forced to withdraw, it will look even more ineffectual.

President Bush's options appear extremely limited, and there is little doubt that the United States will continue to decline as a decisive force in world affairs over the next decade. The real question is not whether U.S. hegemony is waning but whether the United States can devise a way to descend gracefully, with minimum damage to the world, and to itself.

Section 2 International organizations and its role

The Role of Non-state Actors in International Negotiations

In the international cooperation literature, varying roles have been attributed to international and non-governmental organizations. Most of these roles can be placed into three categories: norm generation, enforcement, and negotiations.

Constructivists are most concerned with the dynamics of norm generation and influence. Finnemore and Sikkink (1998) describe a three-stage process in which norms emerge and influence international politics. The first stage of this process is "norm emergence" in which norm entrepreneurs persuade states to accept new norms. As an example of a norm entrepreneur, Finnemore and Sikkink cite Henry Durant's promotion of norms concerning those wounded in war, which eventually culminated in the first Geneva Convention. Both NGOs and international organizations can play integral roles in this process, as they can serve as platforms from which norm entrepreneurs can promote their norms. International organizations can also influence behavior through their use of expertise and information.

The second role attributed to non-state actors involves monitoring compliance and enforcing agreements. Both NGOs and international organizations have an interest in monitoring which states are complying with the agreements they have signed. They can collect information concerning non-compliance, and then make this information known in an attempt to pressure non-complying states to comply. For example, the International Committee of the Red Cross serves in this capacity for the Geneva Conventions. NGOs may not just monitor compliance, but they may succeed in improving compliance levels.

States may find the current level of compliance with agreements to be acceptable, but

NGOs may campaign at both the international and domestic levels through "their technical, organizational, and lobbying skills" for improved levels of compliance (Chayes and Chayes 1993, 204). From the enforcement perspective, the monitoring of compliance by international institutions can reduce the transaction costs associated with enforcing agreements (Keohane 1998).

Rather than focusing on the impetus non-state actors may play in getting issues on the table or in the compliance of agreements, scholars have begun to recognize the roles that non-state actors play in the actual negotiation process. International regimes "deserve greater attention as forums for bargaining rather than primarily as institutions that aid monitoring and enforcement. Interstate bargaining increasingly takes place in the context of international regimes created by states" (Fearon 1998, 298). Participation may come in the form of international organizations providing a forum for bargaining (Morrow 1994; Fearon 1998) or by actual involvement in the intergovernmental debate by international bureaucracies and NGOs (Chayes and Chayes 1993). While negotiators are typically states, "non-state actors participate with increasing frequency in institutional design" (Koremenos, Lipson and Snidal 2001, 763).

This raises the question of whether the participation by non-state actors in negotiations eases or impedes the bargaining process. A number of scholars have pointed to numerous ways in which international institutions have had a positive influence on the process. "Institutions can provide information, reduce transaction costs, make commitments more credible, establish focal points for coordination, and in general facilitate the operation of reciprocity" (Keohane and Martin 1995, p42). Non-state actors may have technical information and expertise that make them well suited for providing credible information to negotiating parties. Martin and Simmons (1998) point to the ability of international organizations to "provide reliable, credible information about the effects of human activities on the environment as a key factor in explaining the success or failure of negotiations on environmental treaties" (p741). Providing information can help to reduce uncertainty, thus providing transparency in negotiations (Keohane 1998).

Transparency in negotiations may ease fears of unequal gain that may rise in negotiating conflicts with distributional implications (Keohane and Martin 1995). By providing a forum for bargaining and communication, regimes can also encourage the exchange of information among its members (Morrow 1994). Besides providing information and encouraging open communication, there are other ways international organizations can reduce transactions costs. Grieco (1990) argues that transaction costs were lowered in GATT negotiations because the participation by the EC reduced the number of actors involved in bargaining.

International organizations can encourage cooperation in negotiations by making issue-linkage and side-payments available (Milner 1992). Martin and Simmons (1998) point to the role international institutions can play in "facilitating or hampering mutually important issue linkages" (p741). Haas (1990) points to the role that the UN played during negotiations of the Mediterranean Plan by using side-payments.

Fearon (1998) argues that international regimes can act at focal points during the negotiation process. "Regimes establish connections and parallels between different rounds of bargaining and may legitimize focal principles because regimes bear legitimacy..." (Fearon 1998, p298). Fearon also argues that these regimes can ease bargaining by placing structure on the bargaining process. When bargaining takes place within the context of an international organization, the rules for negotiations (who can make an offer, when and in what sequence, as well as rules for agreement) may be specified by the regime.

Finally, some scholars have argued that international organizations provide "leadership" in solving problems. Young (1991) focuses on three types of leadership: structural, entrepreneurial, and intellectual and contends that this leadership can make international cooperation more successful through the persuasive manipulation of information and ideas. The entrepreneurial leader, an individual "who relies on negotiating skills to frame issues in ways that foster integrative bargaining," may be representatives of intergovernmental and non-governmental organizations. Intervention in international negotiations by international officials who influence through the manipulation of information, provide impartial mediation, and supply policy expertise has been argued to be highly influential on negotiation outcomes and even crucial for successful negotiations (Haas 1989; Sandholtz and Zysman 1989; Young 1989, 1991).

Young (1989) goes as far as claiming that negotiations will fail in the absence of such leadership. Moravcsik (1999) argues that the role of this leadership is overstated and may even be counterproductive. He argues that states do not have to depend on this supranational leadership because governments have the capacity to collect information and expertise in negotiating. Moravcsik provides evidence from five major European Community treaties, where he argues that states were the major determinants in bargaining, not non-state actors.

Evidence on both sides of this leadership argument has been mainly anecdotal, relying on a few cases. The debate over "leadership" is slightly misplaced. Included in Young's definition of leadership are "structural leaders," individuals representing states.

What needs to be recognized is that regardless of whether negotiators are representatives of states, international organizations or NGOs, they are just that- representatives of these entities. Negotiators do not just do as they please; they are constrained to represent the interests of their state or organization. The role of international organizations and NGOs can be examined in the same way as states - as single, rational actors.

Section 3 Triangle balance of power

(1) The Functions of Regionalism

Two state options offered by economic globalization include either a rejection of nationalism or a rejection of global competition. This has caused some commentators to represent regionalism as being antithetical to globalization. On the other hand, it has also been argued that, rather than being antithetical, globalization and regionalism are in fact complementary processes and that they occur simultaneously and interact. For example, increasing globalization and deregulation associated with a decline in national economic control can induce a 'compensatory' regional process.

However, regionalism can be attractive to states and groups of states for a wide variety of reasons and for a range of social, geopolitical and economic functions. From what has just been said, regionalism can be seen as a form of resistance to globalization and as a mechanism for the consolidation of state power. On the other hand, the opposite can also be true, especially if a central goal of regionalism is economic deregulation. In this sense, regionalism can be said to function in order to facilitate globalization. In the 21st century, it is clear that many problems concerning human survival and/or national development require state cooperation at the regional level. Regionalism thus functions as an appropriate organizing unit for international cooperation at a scale between unworkable global schemes and unsatisfactory national approaches. In other words, regionalism can be seen as possessing an intermediary role between narrowly-defined nationalism and overly-broad globalism. From an economic perspective, some writers refer to attempts to use regionalism as a mechanism to build new institutions which transcend the nation-state in economic contexts as a "strategy of size" built around notions of economic power and economies of scale.

Accepting regionalism on this basis in general ensures that states can have an influence and a distinctive role in solving regional problems within a manageable group. Working in this fashion not only provides a potential mechanism for controlling the behaviour of other regional states, but it also gives the regional group collective power in bargaining with other non-regional states and regions which otherwise would not exist. This invariably means that regionalism is likely to provide member states with a greater degree of security in the broadest sense of the term.

However, while regionalism can potentially fulfill a range of functions at different scales, there exist at least six sources of contestation. First, is the basic issue of whether regionalism is at all considered to be necessary or important. Second, contestation is likely to arise over the type of regionalism which is considered to be the most appropriate. Third, the geographical structure of regionalism is invariably contested — who should be members? who should not?, and so on. Fourth, the goals of the regional grouping are likely to be internally contested. Fifth, states with overlapping regional membership may place themselves in cross-pressured situations which can adversely affect the internal coherence of regional groups due to goal conflicts. Finally, one source of ongoing concern within regional groupings is the extent of member equality. On the one hand, the dominance of one particular state in terms of regional decision-making can be a negative consideration for some member states. On the other hand, incorporating a dominant economic and political power within a regional grouping could facilitate market access and thus be of benefit to smaller states. Such a growth in regional economic interactions in turn might lead to greater regional institutionalization.

This latter point touches on a potentially significant theoretical issue regarding the nature and functions of regionalism. One of the general arguments of Western neorealist is that international economic cooperation is heavily dependent on the presence and efforts of a hegemonic leader. Among other things, the hegemon is seen as playing a key role in sustaining commercial and financial openness. Following this line of argument, we *should* observe regionalism to be developing more fully where a local hegemon is able to create and maintain regional economic institutions. We would also expect that regionalism would advance more slowly in those areas where local hegemonic leadership is less apparent. While the case of the Americas (USA within NAFTA and Brazil within MERCOSUR) may lend some support to this hegemonic leadership hypothesis, the cases of Germany within the EU (not-so-high hegemony with high institutionalization) and Japan within the Asia-Pacific region (high level of hegemony with low level of institutionalization) run counter to this view. In short, outside of the American context, it would appear that the presence of a regional hegemon is neither a necessary nor a sufficient condition for the emergence of successful regional economic or perhaps of any other types of regional institutions.

(2) 21st Century Global Geopolitical Change

As has already been pointed out, the emergence of regionalism can be seen in part as a response to the dynamic processes of globalization. The social science literature has been replete with global geopolitical maps or models purporting to display structures that represent new regional geopolitical realities or which represent the direction of global geopolitical change. Like all such models, not only do they represent ethnocentric and overgeneralised constructions, they are also generally closely allied to present and future global policy needs, desires or intentions on the part of certain individuals, groups or states.

In the 20th century, two simple models were especially influential in describing the global differentiation of space (Figure7-1). During the Cold War period, at the broadest scale, global space was differentiated primarily on ideological grounds — the East (the communist world) and the West (the capitalist world). The over-generalized nature of this model, however, meant that states such as Japan, Australia and New Zealand did not neatly 'fit' this geographical differentiation.

With the demise of the Soviet Union and the end of the Cold War period, the most important basis for the differentiation of global space was on economic grounds (Figure 7-1). Thus, we had the rich states of 'the North' and the poor states of 'the South' (Brandt, 1980). Once again, the Australasian states continued to defy the 'logic' of the overgeneralised model. Perhaps this is why in Wallerstein's core-periphery model, a semi-periphery category needed to be created to accommodate such cases?

This point aside, in essence, both the ideological and the economic models were bipolar models— that is, they are based on oppositions of a geographical duality. The most recently expressed 21st century bipolar model is one in which the duality is much more explicitly related to the nature of globalization. This is Barnett's "functioning core" and "non-integrating gap" (a restated 'neutralized' core-periphery?) model as expressed in his recent book, *The Pentagon's New Map: War and Peace in the Twenty-First Century* (2004). In this book, Barnett draws an extremely arbitrary boundary between those states which are seen to be actively integrated into the global economy — that is, the "functioning core", and the remainder which constitute the "non-integrating gap" (Figure 7-2). While the core states "adhere to globalization's emerging security rule set", the states of the gap apparently do not (Barnett, 2004, p25?6). The gap states are also characterized as being "poor", and as places where life is "nasty", "short", "brutal" and "solitary" (Barnett, 2004, p161?166). Thus, from his map in the Asia-Pacific region, while all of the ASEAN states (including

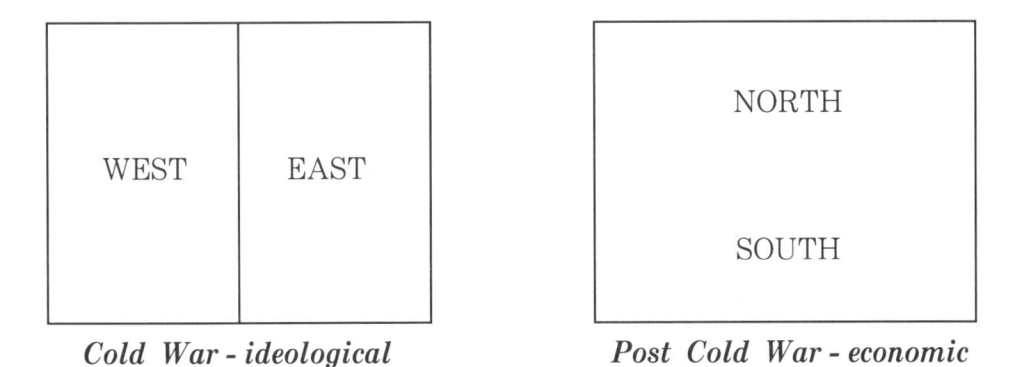

Cold War - ideological   *Post Cold War - economic*

Figure 7-1 Two 20th Century Bipolar Global Pen Region Models

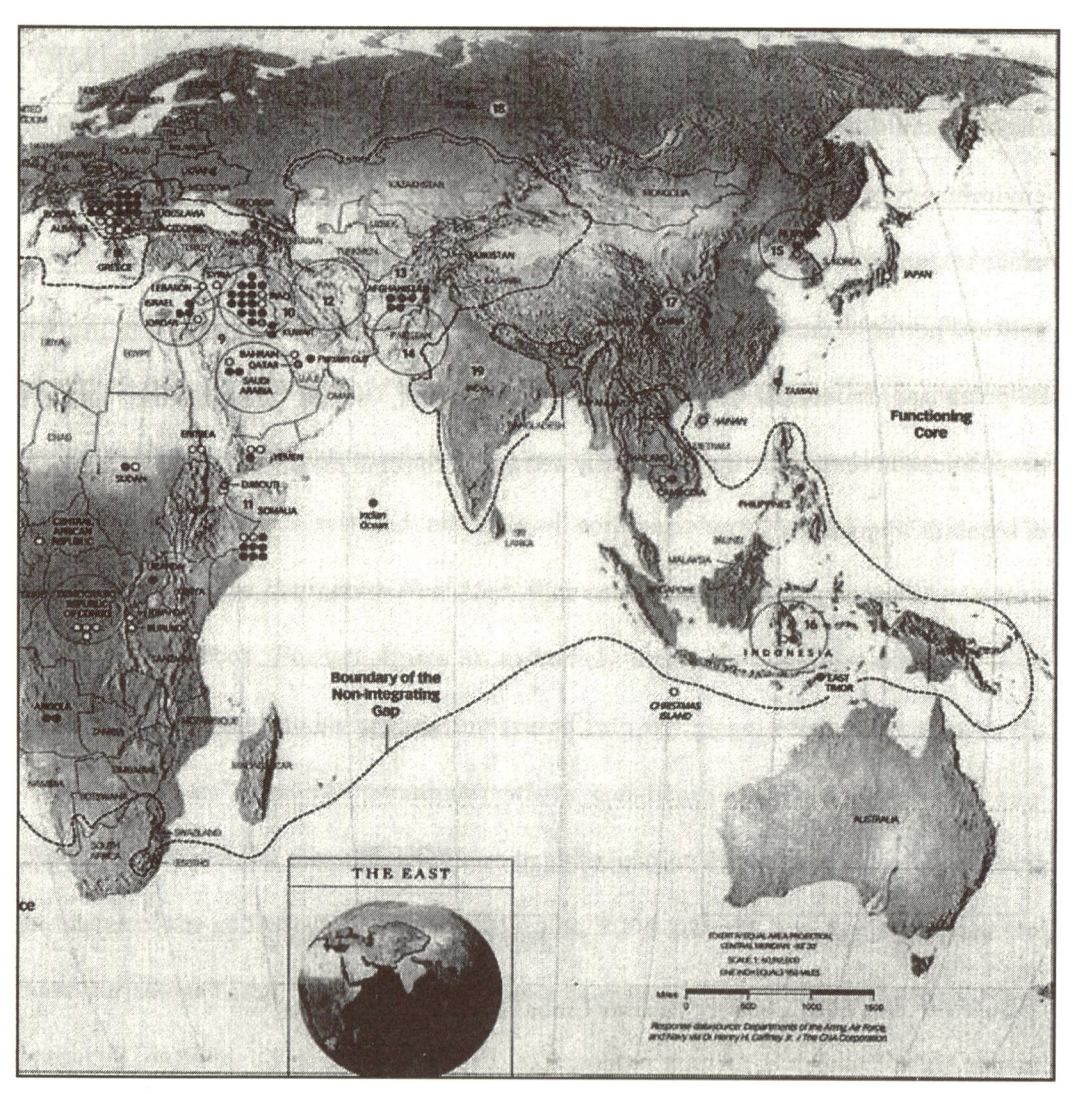

Figure 7-2　The Functioning Core-Non-Integrating Gap Model 8(Barnett, 2004)

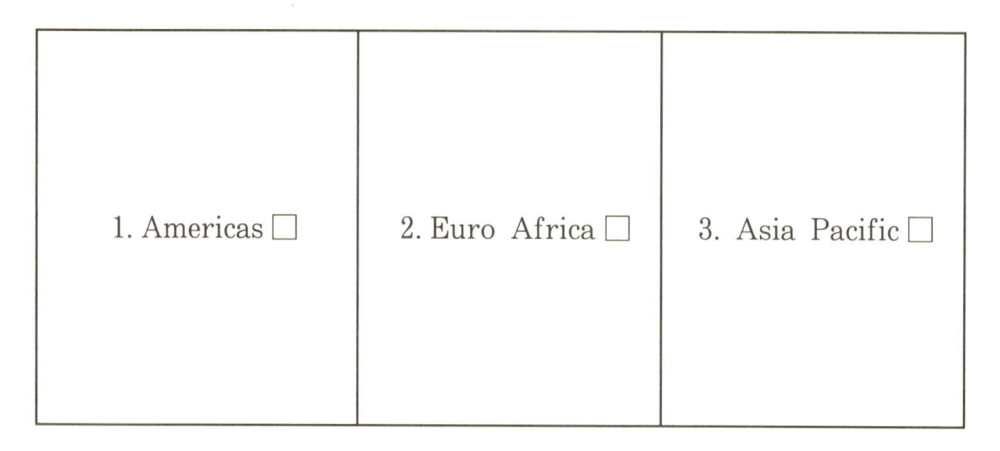

1. Americas ☐	2. Euro Africa ☐	3. Asia Pacific ☐

Figure 7-3　A 21st Century Geopolitical Tri-polar Global Model

Singapore) and Sri Lanka are seen to be located within the non-integrating gap, others, such as North Korea, are portrayed as being part of the functioning core. However, as has been noted elsewhere, Singapore is one of the world's most globalized states. Furthermore, while the Barnett model assumes state homogeneity (in the sense that all parts of a state are seen to be equally 'globalized'), the islands of the Pacific Ocean do not seem to exist at all.

Apart from reasons of simplicity, ethnocentrism and policy orientation, some social scientists are attracted to bipolar global geopolitical models because of their assumed stability — that is, more than two regions (or more than two superpowers) is seen to create a global environment of instability. While others assume that a unipolar model is necessary in order to guarantee stability, yet others argue that the diffusion of global economic and political power to more than two centers inherently affords greater global stability. The tri-polar (or trilateral or tripartite) global model, whose fundamental basis is geopolitical, is seen to be hypothetically attractive to some members of this latter group of scholars (Figure 7-3).

In this tri-polar model, the global differentiation of space is based upon the Americas (pan region1), Euro-Africa (pan region 2) and the Asia-Pacific region. This construction is similar to the German pan region model (Figure 7-4) of the 1940s (O'Loughlin and Van der Wusten, 1990) and to a quasi-Wallerstein model which identifies three core-periphery pan regions (Figure 7-5), each dominated by a Northern core — the USA, EU and Japan — and

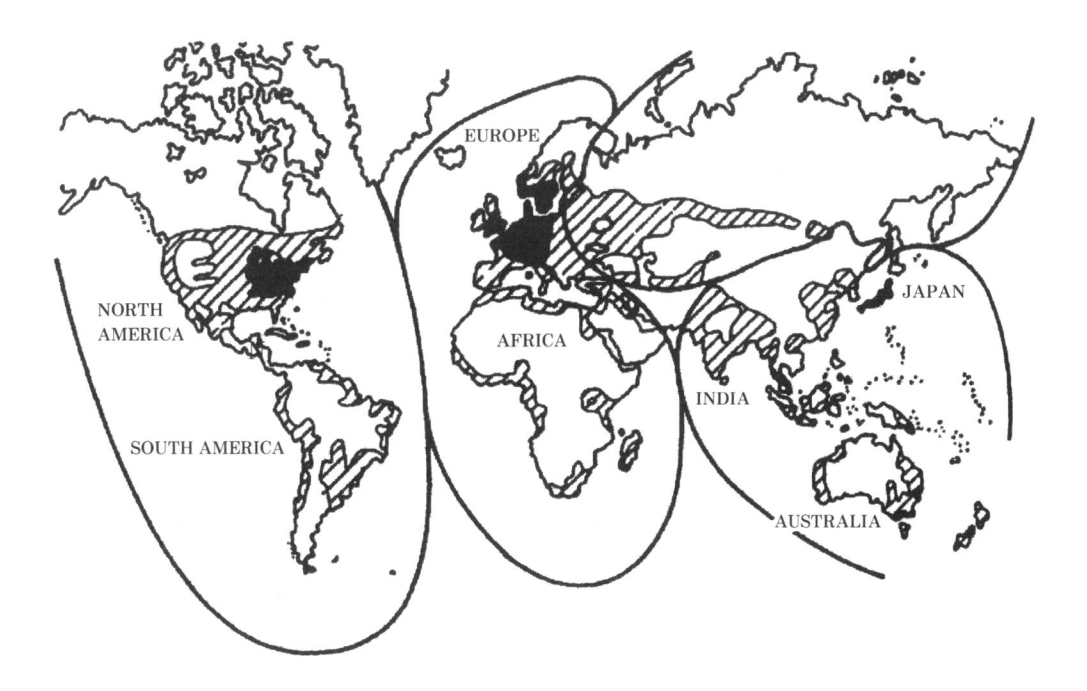

Figure 7-4 Pan Regions of the 1940s (O'Loughlin and Van Der Wusten, 1990)

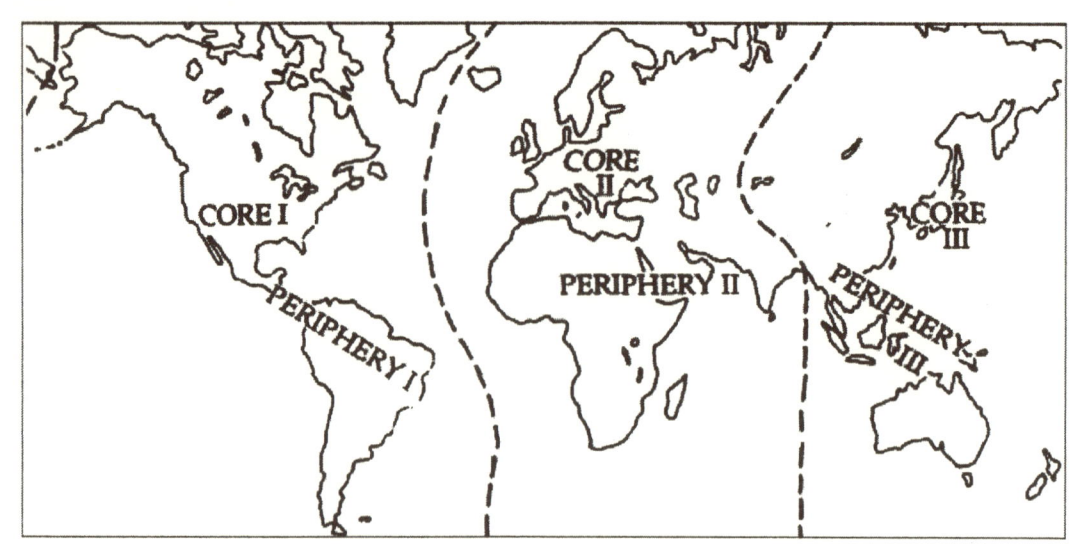

Figure 7-5 Core-Periphery Pan Regions (Peter Taylor, 1993)

containing a Southern periphery. To those living within the Asia-Pacific region and elsewhere favoring neither a uni-polar nor a bipolar model, such a tripartite construction or some other multipolar arrangement possesses inherent appeal.

At least two key issues arise among the wide range of important and interesting questions which can be raised over the tri-polar global geopolitical model. First, is the extent to which attempts have been made by constituent Asia-Pacific states to construct such a model. Second, is the degree to which there is a functional economic and political relationship among constituent states in the Asia-Pacific pan region.

Chapter 8　The future of Asian Regional cooperation

Section 1　Current situation

(1) China-ASEAN FTA

A preparatory Framework Agreement on Comprehensive Economic Co-operation providing for an ASEAN-China Free Trade Area (ACFTA) by 2010 was signed in November 2002 at the Phnom Penh ASEAN Plus Three (APT) summit. It set out an agenda of trade liberalization and facilitation of investment in five areas of economic cooperation. The agreement listed 600 products, mostly agricultural, that were targeted for 'early harvest'[1] tariff reduction by the following year with a commitment to complete negotiations for the remaining 5400 products by June 2004.[2] Satisfied with the progress made by the time of the Vientiane APT Summit in November 2004, the two partners agreed to expedite the implementation of the Early Harvest Program and to provide flexibility to the new Member Countries of ASEAN.[3] ASEAN and China also signed an Agreement on Trade in Goods, an Agreement on Dispute Settlement Mechanism, as well as a Memorandum of Understanding on Transport Cooperation as part of the implementation of the framework agreement.[4]

For some observers, the real significance of ACFTA lies in the simple "10 plus one" integration formula or, "one plus 10", given China's predominance. Thus, unless ASEAN can effectively transform "10 plus one" into "one plus one" through greater ASEAN coherence, it will be overwhelmed by China's rise, especially in the light of its newly established membership of the WTO.[5] Furthermore, by signing the Treaty of Amity and Cooperation, a fundamental document for regional cooperation, during the October 2003 summit in Bali, China began to consolidate its political and economic ties with ASEAN countries and to gain more leverage over them.[6]

However, Japan and South Korea are still cautious about concluding a trilateral free trade agreement with China, despite the signing of a joint declaration on 7 October 2003, in which the leaders of the three nations pledged to bring about closer economic ties.

Both Japan and Korea are worried about China's future move and they both perceive that China aims to grab the initiative for economic integration in the entire Asian region, including ASEAN. However, should the three North Asian countries sign an FTA together with ASEAN, it would create one of the biggest markets in terms of economic power and population and also lead to the East Asian regional integration.

(2) Japan on FTA with ASEAN

China's rapid growth as well as its increasing influence on regional politics in East Asia was evident to some Japanese policy makers since the end of the 1990s.[7] However, the announcement of an agreement between China and ASEAN in November 2002 on the establishment of a FTA within ten years still came as a shock,[8] mainly due to Japan's awareness that it was being left behind. The eagerness to catch up with China's bold approach to ASEAN countries led to proposals such as the "Initiative for Japan-ASEAN Comprehensive Economic Partnership", "Initiative for development in East Asia" and "A community that acts together and advances together", what was called, an "Extended East Asia Community", by Prime Minister Koizumi in Singapore in January 2002.[9]

In November 2002, the Japan-ASEAN summit in Phnom Penh adopted a joint declaration stipulating that both entities would work on a framework of Comprehensive Economic Partnership by 2003 and achieve such partnership within 10 years.[10] The framework was signed into being at the APT Summit in October 2003 with an agreement to begin formal negotiations in 2005 to establish a regional free-trade area by 2012.[11] At the APT Summit in Vientiane in November 2004, Japan welcomed the decision reached by ASEAN leaders to convene the first East Asia Summit (EAS)[12] towards the end of the year 2005. Japan and ASEAN seek a broad-based economic partnership as Japan is the largest investor in ASEAN - approximately US $49.5 billion. Japan considers its policy to be a 'multi-level trading policy'. However, previously different identities seem to lead Japan to contradictory behavior at times, as it tries to act as a leader in the region, while trying to maintain its close political and economic relations with the United States.[13] Hence the initial reluctance of Tokyo to conclude FTAs because of the fear that it could lead to regional protectionism and criticism by Washington. Nevertheless, it has recently accepted the idea as a way to complement multilateral trade liberalization under the WTO and as a strategy to balance worldwide moves in the same direction.

(3) Major Southeast Asian Powers

At the 10th ASEAN summit, leaders of ASEAN and South Korea signed the ASEAN-ROK Joint Declaration on a Comprehensive Cooperation Partnership while affirming that the establishment of an ASEAN-ROK Free Trade Area (AKFTA) would be mutually beneficial. In this regard, they agreed to launch the AKFTA negotiations in 2005 with a goal of having at least 80% of products zero tariff by 2009, and with consideration for special and differential treatment and additional flexibility for new ASEAN Member Countries.

Strategies to achieve economic unity in a common market vary from country to country.

Japan and Singapore are in favor of the creation of FTAs in the region.[14] In contrast, Malaysia does not include the conclusion of such treaties in its concept of integration, though, like South Korea, it favors a broader approach to economic integration that would create a wider range of mutual benefits and supports. China prefers an integration scheme through the China-ASEAN Free Trade Area rather than through bilateral trade agreements. Japan has agreed on the study of a framework to promote trade and investment and to set up a study group on the conclusion of a free trade pact with ASEAN, which observers see this as a bid to compete with China.

ASEAN countries are not "passive" subjects with regard to the competition between Japan and China for predominance over East Asia and are searching for their own independent diplomacy[15] by balancing the two. Most ASEAN policy makers consider Japan to be the key to the economic revitalization their respective countries. Japan's US$ 4.5 trillion economy is almost five times larger than that of China. Hence, Japan is the largest aid donor to ASEAN members in the form of overseas development aid (ODA), which China also receives. In 2000, even after a decade of stagnation, Japanese firms invested US$ 2 billion in ASEAN countries.[16] However, Japan's reluctance to promote freer trade, especially on agricultural products, has been a point of contention.

ASEAN countries, who generally favor of the China-ASEAN FTA, argue that it could make China's huge market accessible for exports from ASEAN countries. It would also upgrade the efficiency of various industries of ASEAN countries through competition in a larger China-ASEAN market. In addition, they welcomed China's voluntary attitude regarding agricultural goods, and expected that it would be easier for them to have access to China's huge market in other sectors as well.

On the other hand, skeptics of the China-ASEAN FTA are concerned that the economies of China and ASEAN would compete with, rather than complement, each other, for instance in attracting investment in the manufacturing sector.[17] They argue that manufacturers of such products as textiles, toys and television sets etc. of ASEAN countries would suffer from an inflow of cheaper Chinese goods. Opponents are also apprehensive that the Chinese government acts not only from economic motives but also from political ones; for example, China's ambition of outmaneuvering Japan from regional leadership.[18] These misgiving about China's influence and the China-ASEAN FTA are particularly strong in Indonesia, Malaysia and the Philippines.

(4) India as a New Element in East Asian regionalization

One emerging and important Asian power is India, who was invited for the first time to attend an APT summit meeting in November 2002. India's approach towards ASEAN countries is considered a new element in the East Asian regional process. New Delhi is ready to consider a free trade agreement with ASEAN. The joint study on AFTA-India linkages for the enhancement of trade and investment recommended the formation of an India-ASEAN Economic Ministers' Meeting (AEM-India) in September 2002.[19] Singapore's Prime Minister Goh Chok Tong reportedly told in the APT summit meeting of November 2002 that ASEAN resembles the body of an airplane with one wing made of East Asia and the other of China and India,[20] enabling the grouping to establish the ASEAN Economic Community by 2020.

Indian and ASEAN officials recently finalized a framework agreement in Jakarta, with a FTA expected to enter into force by 2011. While the products to be included had yet to be decided on, agriculture and textiles were to be excluded pending completion of negotiation on these two critical areas by 2005. India also acceded to the Treaty of Amity and Cooperation (TAC) in Southeast Asia in the 2nd India-ASEAN Summit of October 2003. China signed the TAC at the same time. Moreover, India agreed to conclude a bilateral FTA with Singapore as a long term goal in November 2002 and signed a framework agreement for a Thai-India FTA in October 2003.[21]

(5) **Obstacles to the APT Process**

While the APT process has been progressing rapidly in the last couple of years, there are a number of obstacles to the further development of East Asian regional economic cooperation that involve, among others, the political, economic, cultural and linguistic divisions among the countries of East Asia and the recent severe economic crisis. The following areas stand out for which the APT process might face problems.

Firstly, APT is dependent on the ASEAN regime through which the institutionalization of the APT framework has advanced so far. APT has not yet developed an institutional framework in itself even though East Asian countries are developing the custom of convening to discuss regional issues. For instance, APT's summits are organized, not through an independent institution, but by ASEAN's invitation to China, Japan and South Korea to attend ASEAN meetings.

Secondly, as a consequence of the Asian crisis, the open and liberal approach to foreign relations that had characterized East Asia in the 1990s has been challenged in some countries and differences in approach to economic policy within the region have emerged. Moreover, the institutional diversity of the East Asian region might also limit regional economic cooperation under the APT framework.

Thirdly, major internal problems of the key countries of this region may make it difficult for full attention to be given to issues not directly related to domestic economic welfare and political and social stability, Indonesia being a case in point. Japan has grappled with its stagnant economy and may find that regional issues will receive less priority. Thus, how much of their resources or time the APT members may devote to foreign policy issues, such as driving the APT process forward, depends on the capability of the member states to manage domestic problems.

Despite the clear evidence about both the impact that highly mobile capital flows have had in precipitating and intensifying the East Asian crisis, there has been little serious attempt to curb such initiative or establish different, especially East Asian regulatory regimes. There are also formidable technical obstacles to the currency swap arrangements, particularly given the lack of governmental capacity amongst some of Southeast Asia's less developed countries.[22] The Chiang Mai Initiative (CMI) of 2000, which was designed to promote regional financial crisis management, is notable in this regard, because while it may have had a symbolic importance, it has been of little practical implementation so far.[23]

Fourthly, cooperation among APT members might be constrained by conflicting interests among the APT members. Both Japan and China are competitors and have regional leadership aspirations. In this context it is required to distinguish between the financial and 'real' economies to understand the potential obstacle to the development of an encompassing regional policy position, and the inherent conflict of interest between region's wealthier and poorer states it reveals. International economic activities are becoming footloose, stateless and geared to transnational regulatory framework.[24]

Fifthly, at the level of the real economy, the distinctive structure of East Asian business and the close relations between economic and political elites makes reform more visible, and resistance to change being more pronounced and the incentives for regional cooperation to protect broadly similar regional political and economic structures carry more weight. The conclusion of intra-regional agreements that have the capacity to accommodate powerful domestic constituencies becomes easier to understand in this context. In addition, as John Ravenhill notes, preferential trade agreements may have symbolic importance that go beyond their economic worth as they help to consolidate underlying regional relations.[25] APT members have been negotiating a series of bilateral FTAs, as for instance, Singapore and Japan in January 2002. South Korea is also negotiating FTAs with other countries.

However, the fact that these trade initiatives in East Asia are happening predominantly at the bilateral level, or have been attached to existing structures like AFTA, is a major obstacle to the development of region-wide agreements of a sort that could give greater credibility to the APT process.

Sixthly, the U.S. remains a major player in this region as a member of APEC who is committed to ensuring an open global economy that is not segmented along regional lines.

The U.S government's prime concern with combating international terrorism could also bring pressure to bear on such APT members as Japan and South Korea to hold back the development of East Asian regionalization. Furthermore if the U.S. considers APT as a way of allowing China to exert a greater influence in East Asia, it may decide to try to forestall any attempts to increase regional cooperation there.[26] Thus the effect of American influence in East Asia appears to vary across issue areas. While American intervention in the region's post-crisis development had the effect of accelerating the regional political and economic cooperative approach, the United States' "war on terror" has revealed deep fault-lines across the region. In such circumstances it is obvious that East Asian countries should develop a region-wide response to American actions through the APT process though it is very difficult at the moment and the prediction holds that APT will continue to be influenced by American actions.

Section 2 Chinese financial instability

(1) Bad Debt

China's financial system continues to be burdened by a mountain of non-performing loans (NPLs) in the state banking system, despite government promises to take action to reduce it. In its annual report on global debt released on May 3, the accounting firm Ernst & Young highlighted the dangers of China's bad debt, estimated at a staggering $US911 billion.

According to the report, China's current NPL level was equal to 40 percent of gross domestic product (GDP). It was almost twice the 2002 figure of $480 billion, and larger than the country's foreign currency reserves of $875 billion-the world's biggest. The four major state-owned commercial banks accounted for $358 billion of bad loans-almost three times the officially reported figures. "With the exception of China, every market covered in 2004 report has witnessed a reduction in its levels of NPLs written before 1997," it stated.

The alarming report came just before an initial public offering (IPO) of shares worth $9.9 billion by the Bank of China in Hong Kong. China's central bank-the People's Bank of China-posted an angry statement on its website attacking the report as "ridiculous and barely understandable" and damaging to the "image" of China's banking assets.

Ernst & Young prepared the report as part of its efforts to explore new potential in the trading of NPLs in the international financial markets. The firm claimed that its higher estimation of Chinese bad debt was based on access to broader information, including the rapid growth of loans in recent years and details of distressed debt companies (such as rural credit cooperatives) attached to major banks. These had been excluded from previous reports.

Under pressure from Beijing, Ernst & Young withdrew its report last weekend, declaring it had been in error and promised that "such an embarrassing situation will not happen again". The firm now accepts the official figure of $133 billion for the bad debt of the Big Four state banks, saying the estimate is "based on objective evidence of impairment". Ernst & Young currently has a lucrative contract to audit the Industrial & Commercial Bank, one of the Big Four and China's largest lender, ahead of its overseas share listing in September.

The incident revealed Beijing's extreme sensitivity to any comment critical of its financial system. Even if the official estimate of the bad debts of the four leading state banks is correct, which is unlikely, other issues raised in the Ernst & Young report-including surging lending, investment bubbles and the transfer of bad assets to other state companies-remain unanswered.

According to the *Financial Times* on May 4, the Ernst & Young report is line with a number of recent studies, including by the corporate consultancy firm, McKinsey, released in the same week. "While there have been improvements in the banking sectors, and the government has sought to address NPLs, the core causes for the build-up have not been fully dealt with," the McKinsey report stated. "Until these problems are addressed, the problem is likely to persist, and the banking system will remain vulnerable to potential liquidity shocks."

Prior to his firm's retraction, Jack Rodman, managing director of Ernst & Young, commented: "I think the numbers will be a big surprise because China has been giving the impression [with its banks listing overseas] that the problem is behind us. China has not really resolved the issue-they have just moved it from one state enterprise to another."

International investors are concerned because China is due to open up its banking system at end of this year under the terms of its entry into the World Trade Organization (WTO). Since 2005, major global banks and financial institutions have invested billions of dollars in the large Chinese state banks.

More broadly, China is one of the main growth engines for the world economy. Its central bank is playing a leading role along with its Asian counterparts in purchasing the US dollar-dominated assets and financing the huge US deficits. China's continuing expansion of around 9 percent a year has stimulated the Asia-Pacific economies and lifted the world's commodities prices to unprecedented levels.

The growth of massive bad debts in China's banking system has exposed the fact that this apparently strong economic performance is resting on shaky financial foundations.

The Beijing government claims to have cleared $560 billion in bad debts since 1999 and injected fresh capital into the major state banks from the central bank's foreign currency reserves. Now it is clear that much of this "reduction" has been through transfers to other state-owned disposal agencies, and nullified by surges in new lending.

Up to last December, the Chinese government had placed more than $330 billion of bad debts from the four major state banks in asset management firms. The four largest firms-Cinda, Orient, Great Wall and Huarong-still have $230 billion in bad debts to dispose of. China's finance ministry continues to guarantee bonds valuing hundreds of billions of dollars issued to the state banks when the bad assets were transferred.

In other words, bad assets have been transferred from one state sector to another, but the financial system as a whole continues to be weighed down by huge levels of bad debt, with the Chinese government as the ultimate debtor.

Moreover, from 2002 to 2004, the Big Four also contributed more to the country's investment bubble by making $225 billion in new risky loans-one-third in real estate. Chinese banking authorities attempted to obscure the nature of these loans by classifying them as of "special mention".

For instance, the China Construction Bank, which was listed on the Hong Kong share market last year, reported an acceptable bad loan ratio of just 3.8 percent. But it had to admit that its ratio of "special mention" loans to overall loans was a high 8 percent.

(2) Interest rate rise

Beijing managed to pressure Ernst & Young into modifying its estimate of bad debts. On April 27, however, the Chinese central bank suddenly lifted its benchmark one-year lending rate by 0.27 percent to 5.85 percent in a tacit admission of concern about the rising tide of bank lending.

The IMF has warned that China needs further interest rate increases in order to slow down the "over-invested" sectors, especially property. At the same time, the IMF, in line with Washington's demands, called on China to use its current account surplus, which is likely to remain at about 7 percent of GDP this year, to implement a "flexible" exchange rate with the dollar.

The Chinese government is walking a fine line. Further interest rates rises could also result in higher levels of bad debt. Most Chinese enterprises, particularly small and medium manufacturing firms, operate on thin profit margins and are already under pressure due to the rising costs of raw materials and even labor. Overcapacities in industries like steel, cement and textile are already threatening to undermine profits.

The most serious speculative bubble is in real estate, where prices had been driven up by the prospects of Yuan revaluation and the 2008 Beijing Olympic Games. Chinese central bank statistics at the end of 2005 show that property lending reached 3.07 trillion Yuan (about $379 billion) or nearly 17 percent of the GDP. The National Bureau of Statistics recently warned that unsold residential space across the country had risen by 23.8 percent to 123 million square meters by the end of March, as compared to last year. Any collapse of the property bubble could have catastrophic consequences for the country's fragile banking system.

China's economic expansion cannot go on indefinitely. Speculative investment and mounting levels of bad debts are the inevitable result of the Chinese government's policies designed to maintain huge inflows of foreign investment and high economic growth rates.

The December issue of the *Far East Economic Review* pointed out that China's ability to attract 10 times more foreign capital than rival India, was based not on cheaper labor, but on more efficient infrastructure. China has invested $24 billion a year to upgrade highways, compared to India's major $16 billion road project over eight years. Electricity prices for industrial users in China are half those in India. In 2003, 61 percent of Indian factories had to buy their own power generator, compared to just 27 percent in China. Chinese exports to the US take 3-4 weeks on average to reach their destination, compared to 7-12 weeks from India.

China's state-directed investment in infrastructure has been vital to attracting foreign investment, but is fraught with difficulties. Provinces and cities compete with each other for investment by building their own ports or industrial parks. The process has led to widespread duplication and overcapacity. The local branches of state banks function as sources of cheap credit and inevitably bear the burden of failed infrastructure projects. According to the World Bank, about one-third of China's fixed asset investment in infrastructure in the 1990s was wasted. Few bank officials have been held accountable.

At the same time, the anarchic economic growth has led to growing social inequalities. In order to prevent unemployment from rising, the government maintains inefficient state-owned enterprises, which account for more than 70 percent of the mainly state bank loans. Their output has fallen to just a quarter of the GDP in the past decade. Beijing fears any fire-sale style privatization of the state sector, which has already laid off over 30 million workers, would threaten social stability. The Chinese central bank admitted in 2000-2001 that "politically-directed" bank lending accounted for 60 percent of bad loans.

Nor can Beijing afford politically to rein in foreign investment and economic growth. An Asian Development Bank (ADB) study last month demonstrated that China has needed higher and higher rates of growth to generate jobs. In the 1980s, a 3 percent economic growth rate generated 1 percent increase in employment. Because of higher productivity, however, China needed nearly 8 percent in annual growth in the 1990s to create the same job growth rate. This year it is estimated that 25 million people will enter the labor market, but only 11 million will find a job.

One result of these economic policies is a systemic build-up of huge levels of bad debt that threatens to trigger a major financial crisis with reverberations around the world. Far from being a demonstration of the viability of pro-market policies, China could well prove to be an Achilles heel of global capitalism.

Section 3 Security problem

(1) Stabilization under Uni-polar Structure Led by U.S.

The present security environment in North-East Asia is maintained. In a barely stability under the uni-polar structure led by the U.S. with the strong military power. Also, Japanese contribution in the economy and technology to this area has been very remarkable. The figure8-1 is the general composition of this situation. Four nations of Japan, U.S.,

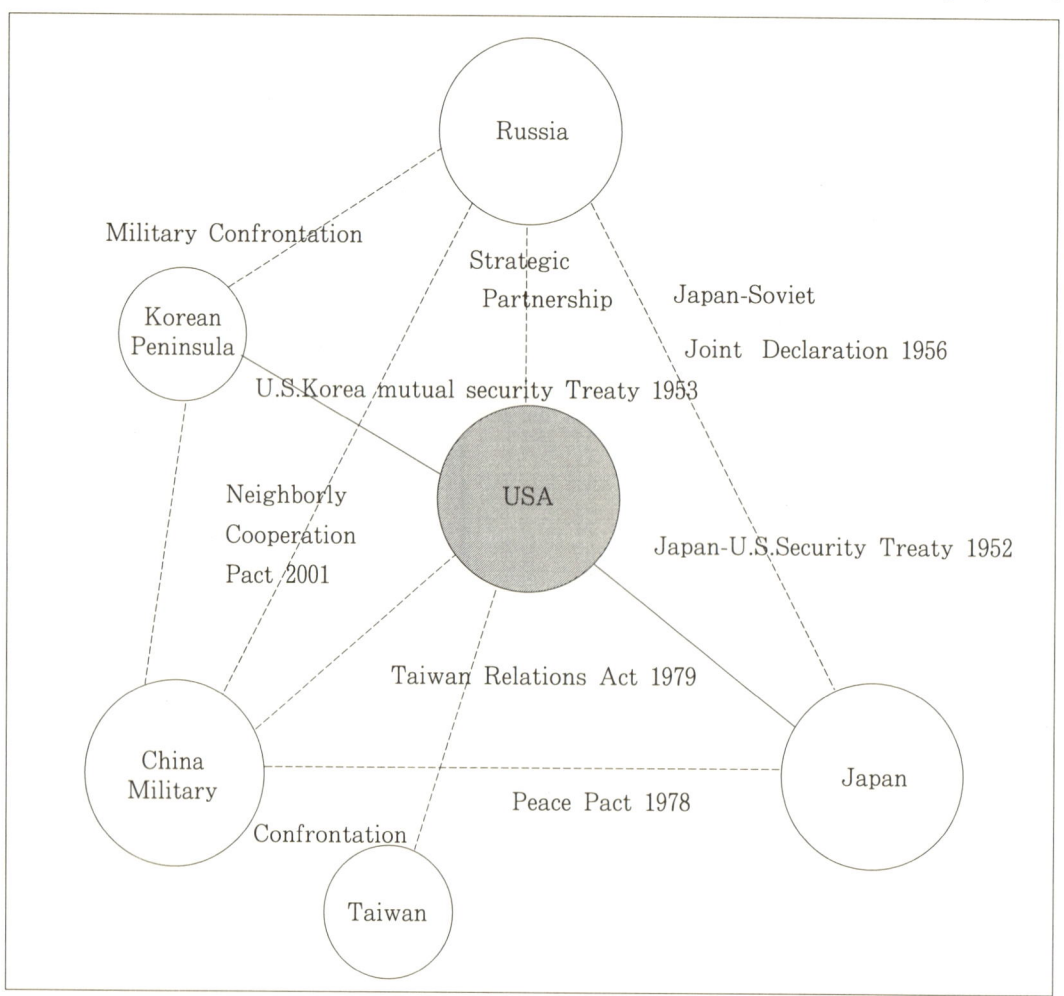

Figure 8-1 International Relations in the Present North-East Asia

China and Russia are maintaining with each other stabilized international relations for the time being. Japan and the U.S. have the firmest relation in the Japan-US Security Treaty. Subsequently, South Korea is joined militarily by U.S.-South Korea mutual defense pact. China and Russia have concluded the strategic partnership with the U.S. in a light friendly relation. However, the recent U.S.-China relationship is becoming troubled because the U.S. specifies China as a strategic competitor. On the other hand, the China-Russia good neighbor friendship cooperation treaty was concluded in 2001 as the countervailing measure to the U.S. Moreover, the active approach to the Korean Peninsula by China and Russia is recently becoming marked.

Reason for Stable Security Environment in North-East Asia

   a. Devastating Breakdown of Soviet Armed Forces

The greatest change in the Japanese security environment in the post-Cold War decade is that the military threat from Far East Russia was gone. In these ten years, the Far East Russian armed forces decreased from 500,000 and 40 divisions to 110,000 and 10 divisions. Moreover, feeling the threat for eastern expansion of NATO, Russia has refrained from taking positive action in the Far East, based on their traditional strategy to avoid two-sided confrontation.

On the other hand, Japan has provided financial assistance of a total of 6,300 million dollars in the communication and energy related project to Russia. This economical support may be an assistance not to be lost for Russia which gives top priority to economic reconstruction for some time in the future. Although, Japan and Russia declared the termination of state of war by the "Japan-Soviet Joint Declaration" in 1956, the territorial problem between Japan and Russia is still unsolved.

   b. U.S. Deterrence of Crisis

In North-East Asia, there are two crisis areas involving the military confrontation, namely the Korean Peninsula and the Taiwan Strait.

In the Korean Peninsula, although there is the cease-fire agreement concluded in 1953, there has been no peace treaty. Legally speaking, the state of war is still continuing for 50 years in this area. Although the strained situation does not improve still, the gap of national powers including the military strength between the South Korea and the North Korea have been increasing. While Russia has refrained from the arms transfer to North Korea, the U.S. has positively provided South Korea with many newest arms. Moreover, South Korean economy has grown remarkably. Furthermore, the presence of the 36,000 U.S. Forces in South Korea and the 38,000 U.S. Armed Forces in Japan, the sunshine policy and international food aid to the North Korea have deterred the full-scale military invasion by the North Korea.

China firmly maintains the policy that reserves the military power use in cases of Declaration of Independence by Taiwan and foreign intervention. However, Taiwan has done its best in armed forces modernization, such as acquiring modern arms system in these ten years. As a result, Taiwan can maintain qualitative predominance in equipment of land, sea and air to China by 2005. Moreover, the U.S. participation to Taiwan by based on the Taiwan Relating Act makes difficult military power solution of the Taiwan problem by China.

c. China Concentrating on National-Power Reinforcement

Present China does its best in consistent modernization of economy and the military strength, and is concentrating on national-power reinforcement. However, the characteristics of China like the Communism, nationalism and ambition to be a great power will not change significantly in the future. China that aims at a superpower in the 21st century is in the transition stage now, and the success or failure will be in a fifty-fifty chance. Because, the recent affiliation with the WTO demands improvement of competition of many companies in the international market, and the 2008 Olympic Games requires a large amount of capital for infrastructure development. Moreover, there is social unrest, such as serious joblessness, unbalance of the economic structure, and an ethnic minority's pressure. These increase the uncertainty of Chinese society's future.

Characteristics of Threat to Japan in post-Cold War

The threat to Japan in the Cold War age was, first and last, a landing invasion by the Soviet Union to the Japanese northern areas, but the Japanese security environment in post-Cold War is comparatively stable as described in (1). However, it can only be regard as a temporary phenomenon, because today's threats to Japan are indirect and potential.

a. Indirect Threat

The threat from the North Korea in the Korean Peninsula is surely deterred by the South Korean and the U.S. Forces at the northern area of Seoul and the U.S. Forces' prompt reinforcement from Japan and CONUS. The strain in Taiwan Strait is maintaining the present stable condition by the Taiwan armed forces that are qualitatively predominant, and the U.S. Seventh Fleet that can respond immediately according to the circumstances. In these two crisis areas in North-East Asia, outbreak of crises by the two barriers, namely the interested states' forces and the U.S. Forces. In short, the security environment of today's Japan is not the situation in which a threat reaches Japan directly. So, the U.S. will demand a positive support by Japan in case of emergency in the surrounding areas. Also, if international relations change, these indirect threats to Japan may change suddenly to direct threats.

b. Potential Territory and Resources Problem

60% or more of the past causes of war were territory or resources problem. Japan has three territorial problems: the northern 4 islands, Takeshima Island and the Senkaku Islands. Also the fishing and seabed-resources problems based on the oceanic laws exist around these islands. These concerned countries are Russia, the North and the South Korea, China, and Taiwan. Illegal occupation of northern 4 islands and Takeshima Island is actually carried out by their constituted authorities, and the invasion to the Senkaku Islands is repeated by Chinese. However, by the reduction of Russia military strength and the other countries' military confrontation with each other, these problems happen to be in potential state.

(2) Destabilization by Multi-polar Structure −Probable Change by around 2030−

The uni-polar structure led by the U.S. in the present North-East Asia will continue for some term if the national power building of Russia and China is delayed or failed, and the two crisis areas, the Korean Peninsula and the Taiwan Strait, especially the former, remain as they are. However, these conditions can change drastically by several factors such as the

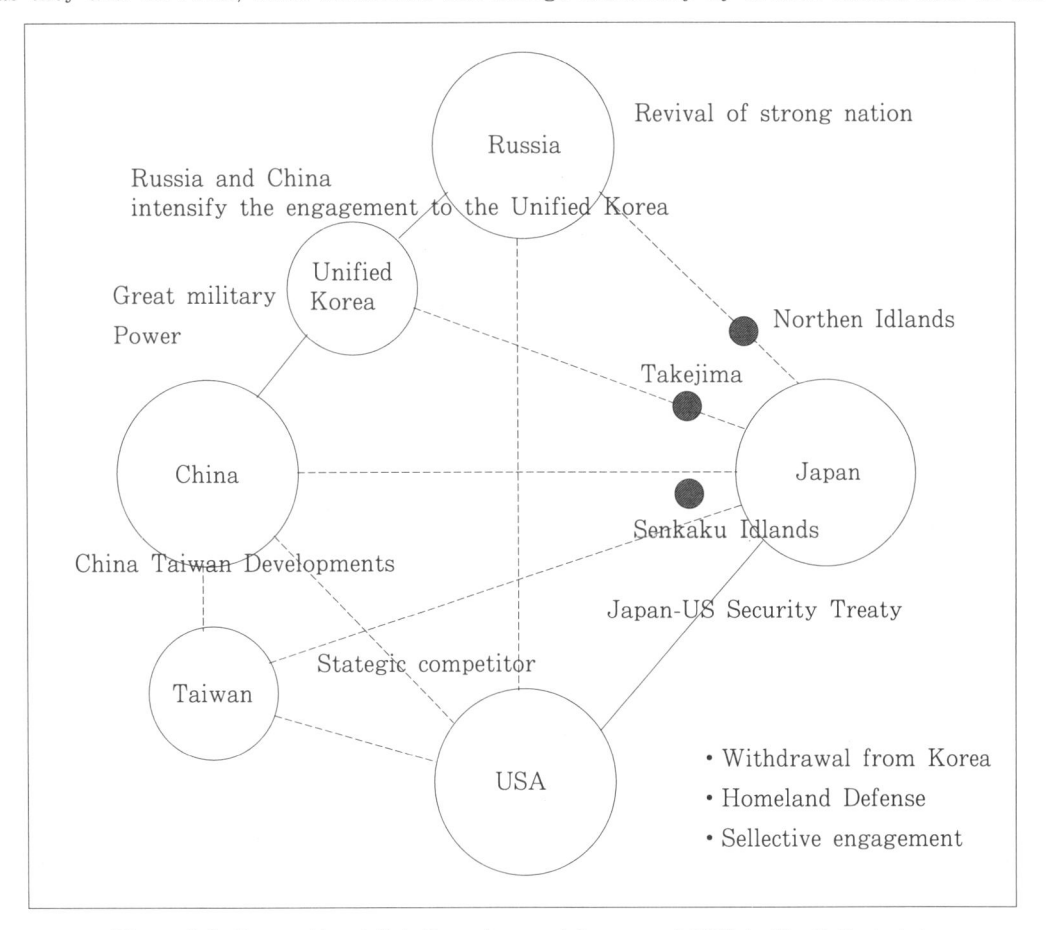

Figure 8-2 International Relations Assumed by around 2030 in North-East Asia

degree of cooperation of Russia and China, the situational developments between China and Taiwan, the rapidity of change of the political, economical and social situations in the North Korea, and the trend of public opinion in South Korea. Above all, the unification of the Korean Peninsula will have a much greater impact on the change of the international relations in North-East Asia.

I believe that this opportunity will come before long with high probability, because there are many triggers such as ① Kim Jong-Il who is now absolute ruler will become aged, ② the food shortage and aggravation of economy situation in the North Korea will grow worse than now, ③ political refugee's rapid increase, ④ the South Korean sunshine policy, ⑤ the positive intervention to the Korean Peninsula by China and Russia.

When Korea is unified, the U.S. Forces in South Korea will probably have to be withdrawn because of the opposition by China, Russia and the new Korea. Accordingly, the U.S. will have to tone down her commitment in North-East Asia from serious engagement to that of forward military deployment. At that time, the uni-polar structure led by the U.S. come to an end, and the multi-polar structure will be built up by the U.S., Russia, China and Japan in North-East Asia as shown in Fig. -2. Consequently, these four nations will repeatedly act either harmoniously or in the check- and- balance manner each other, and the power balance in this area will become unstable.

(3) **Moves of Main Powers by 2030**

a. U.S. Forces Withdrawal from Korean Peninsula

It can be said that the U.S. Forces presence in the South Korea is a symbolic existence for active control of security in North-East Asia. The North-South military confrontation in the Korean Peninsula can may even be convenient for the U.S. global security strategy. In that context, the U.S. Forces withdrawal from the Korean Peninsula is the critical turning point for the U.S. to convert the security strategy in North-East Asia.

Originally, the U.S. people have a subconscious mind which to return to the Monroe Doctrine, dropping out of the world and aiming at the growth of national power.

We can surmise it from several cases as below. The expression of "the maintenance of 100,000 personnel forward presence in East Asia" has been deleted from the Defense Annual Report 2001. The QDR 2001 has made it appear that the acceptance of a policy giving priority to the homeland defense, the implementation of NMD program and the emphasis of mobility capability in the U.S. military transformation. As a result, the U.S. Asian strategy will be back away from the North-East Asia's top priority at the present time. It will be highly possible that the U. S. adopt selective and partial engagement on the occasion of a future crisis in North-East Asia.

b. Russia: Reversion to Ancient Regime?

It is believed that the latest Russian politics turn to the direction of strong central management organization like the former Soviet Union. Its Security Council has been reformed so that the core persons are made up of the KGB graduates to fulfill a role as the national power structure. In Russia, it is a dominant characteristic to return to the one-party dictatorship by President Putin and nationalism. Moreover, Russian national security concept in 2000 emphasizes to the achievement of their national interest and the incremental growth of a military threat to Russia. This concept is also written clearly that chief threat from outside was "the territory return demand". It gives suggestions so that Russia adopts the hard attitude to the Northern Territories issue with Japan.

Russia concluded Russia-China good neighbor friendship cooperation treaty in 2001. Also, the "Shanghai cooperation mechanism" was founded as a place of extensive deliberations such as security, economy, culture, etc. by five the nations of Russia, China, Kazakhstan, Kyrgyz, and Tajikistan. China is the best customer of Russia as an arms market. Accordingly, the future bilateral relation will increasingly be strengthened. Russia is now progressing to strengthen ties with Vietnam and the North Korea which were once allies, in arms export and nuclear technical cooperation.

In the opinion poll of Japanese Ministry of Foreign Affairs in March 2001,"Russia is a threat, or can become a future threat" scored a total of 61%, and "it not being a threat" was 21.9%. For the Japanese, the vast quantity of the conventional arms and the nuclear weapons which Russia possesses, under loose management and the corrupt bureaucrat in the government and the military are serious concern matter on Japanese security.

c. China Moves to External Expansionism

Chinese political, economical and social situations in 20-30 years will not be any more transparent than the present. The Communist Party dictatorship in Chinese political situation will not change, by the way of educating the young directors of the Communist Party doctrine and the theory of Marxism, contrary to internationalization of the economy. Although economic growth will continue, the gap of the wealth and poverty between the coastal area and the other areas may increase, and the social unrest may escalate. Such bilateral character in politics, economy, and society is the unstable factor, so that we cannot decide whether China will become strong state or not.

Meanwhile, the policy of military strength modernization will be unchanged, to keep introducing advanced arms in accordance with the principles of going high-tech and making powerful armed forces. Consequently, it will be clear that China-Taiwan military balance converts to the China predominance after several years. Moreover, there will be concern that China may move to the external expansionism by its modernization of Navy and Air Force, and its military strategy. There are two distinctive features in the Chinese military strategy. The first is that they will solve by arms the sovereignty issues including territorial rights. The second is that the so-called "second islands line" (Ogasawara Islands, Mariana Islands, Guam, Parao) is included in the sea area of the Chinese naval activity. Accordingly, if China holds Taiwan Straits under her power in the near future, most of sea lanes of Japan will lapse into their hegemony.

In addition, although it is an uncertain information, the main enemy for China in the near future is clearly written to be Japan in the paper which the Shanghai international strategy society in August, 1999 submitted to the Chinese government.

d. Anxiety About Unified Korea

When unified Korea was born in some way, there are the following three apprehensive problems for the Japanese security. The first is the kind of organization and character the political power chooses. That is, whether it is a perfect unified state, or one state with two systems as we call a mosaic state, or another form. The second is the whereabouts of the international relationship between the unified Korea and the U.S., Japan, China and Russia. The third is how to reconstruct the economic strength that will decline someday, and how to treat the huge military strength containing WMD.

The worst form in these choices for Japan is the birth of a political power of anti-American and anti-Japanese, with the economic dislocation, the growing nationalism and a large military power. Because, it is highly possible that such incidents take place as the demand for apology for the past for economical support, espionage activities and terrorism by the resident from Koreans in Japan, and intimidation and occupancy of Takeshima island by military power, and so on.

(4) Changing Threat Aspect to Japan

a. Direct and Obvious Threats

Two barriers mentioned above will be lost when the birth of unified Korea and certain degree of development in the Taiwan issue become actual events. Then, the threat from Russia, the Korean Peninsula, and China will actualize directly to Japan. Japan has the unresolved territorial and resource issues with these nations. Also, there are several problems about the liquidation of the past such as historical perception and compensation between Japan and China or the new Korea.

b. Diverse and Complex Threats

The threat in the future will entirely change the aspect. Its characteristics are diversity, complexity and simultaneity. For instance, diplomatic negotiations and military operations will take place at the same time, with coexistence of external aggression with the internal rebellion or NEO in the belligerent nation. Also, in the military affairs, there is a co occurrence of an invasion by a regular forces and an asymmetric threat such as terrorism, guerilla or WMD.

Especially for Japan with thousands of detached islands, the geographical characteristic is easy to come down surprise attack. Besides, the poor national crisis management system and the inadequate national emergency legislation in Japan are apt to induce such a contingency.

Section 4   Monetary system

(1) **The Problem of an Asian Monetary Union**
The new enthusiasm for regional cooperation, followed by the financial crisis, sparked a number of fanciful financial proposals of which one was the idea of a common East Asian currency. Hong Kong first proposed an Asian monetary union in 1999 and subsequently suggested a common currency for Hong Kong and Singapore as a first step. ASEAN's Hanoi Plan of Action of 1998, its comprehensive statement in response to the crises, called for a study of the feasibility of an ASEAN currency. However, such an idea is clearly premature so that some of its staunchest advocates quickly retreated.[27]

Thus regional monetary cooperation in East Asia is likely to be more difficult to construct than cooperation in trade. In Europe, monetary union followed decades after trade liberalization. The strict Maastricht requirements that governments have to meet to qualify for participation in the Euro indicate the extent to which monetary integration intrudes into domestic policy-making autonomy. Collaboration in monetary terms poses more of a threat to sovereignty than does trade integration.

The difficulty that the ASEAN economies have found with monetary collaboration is reflected in the APT process. One of the ironies of the recent crisis was that the seeming imperative for regional collaboration on financial issues, which ultimately would require greater use of regional currencies, was contradicted by the lesson that East Asian countries that had maintained some forms of capital controls were best able to escape the most damaging effects of the crisis. Moreover, APT's adherence to the 'ASEAN way' of consensus and voluntarism, like ASEAN and APEC, and lingering concerns about establishing a powerful secretariat that might ultimately threaten national autonomy are also likely to make the development of an effective monetary union more difficult.[28] Yet East Asian countries under the APT process, with few exceptions such as Myanmar, have acted to increase levels of interdependence, not the reverse, despite the many obstacles within the process itself.[29] In neoliberal and liberal terms, institutionalization reduces transaction costs, creates a sense of mutual interests and socializes parties in cooperative habits. The increased trust and cooperative habits that liberal theories expect to become entrenched through cooperation would not be expected in East Asia if concrete outcomes are important.[30] Thus the region is clearly different, though not the polar opposite in terms of institutionalization, from Europe, with a unique regional cooperation pattern that creates many obstacles to the institutionalization of the APT process in practice.

(2) **Prospects of the APT Process**

Despite the obstacles discussed these countries might be able to overcome those constraints that would lead to the steady emergence of the APT as a regional cooperative arrangement. Observers contend that a process of enhanced cooperation between the ASEAN members and China, Japan and South Korea could build confidence over time and erode long-held animosity and distrust. Japan and China seem to have understood the basic need to deepen the institutionalization of APT, and although they are likely to compete fiercely, neither country wishes to stall this highly dynamic region-wide endeavor. Moreover there is an issue of reciprocity in the process. A factor that binds the members of the APT process is their remaining capacity for economic growth; with the exception of Japan, who needs the exports and resource markets of neighboring countries to fuel fresh growth. Furthermore the regional liquidity fund that is slowly evolving will give the members of APT greater autonomy in crises.

Although East Asian countries are diverse, the progress of APT lies in a number of commonalities - 'ASEAN values', common institutions, a distinctive brand of capitalism, the experience of warfare and the urge for deeper economic integration - all of which provide APT with a potential basis for regional identity and consolidation and result in a successful regional institution. The various kinds of cooperation and coordination currently occurring within the APT regional framework could grant the APT process success in becoming a dominant regional organization in East Asia.

The leaders of ASEAN and Northeast Asian countries are willing to explore the phased evolution of APT into an East Asian Summit (EAS), as well other for a as tools of enhancing cooperation in East Asia, as long as they do not undermine the strategic importance and relevance of ASEAN in the overall framework for cooperation. Therefore, EASs must be conducted through a gradual and building block approach to ensure ASEAN's capacity to ensure the whole process.

The Vientiane APT summit of November 2004 noted, among others:
- the establishment of the APT Unit in the ASEAN Secretariat and assistance of the Plus Three countries to it.

- the steady progress in ASEAN+3 cooperation, especially in monetary, financial and economic sectors, with a speedy implementation of all measures aimed at broadening and deepening East Asia cooperation encouraged.
- the need to develop the Asian Bond Market
- the need to combat emerging diseases through new mechanisms, such as the establishment of "Outbreak Response Teams".
- the establishment of an East Asia Free Trade Area (EAFTA) and the decision by APT Economic Ministers to set up a feasibility study on EAFTA.

The Leaders of the Plus Three countries supported ASEAN Leaders' decision to convene the first East Asia Summit (EAS) in Malaysia in 2005 and reaffirmed the role of APT process, with ASEAN as the major driving force, as the main vehicle for the eventual establishment of an East Asian Community.[31]

(1) "Early Harvest Program" refers to a unilateral reduction in customs duties by China on imports from ASEAN countries.

(2) ASEAN Secretariat (2002). Framework Agreement on Comprehensive Economic Cooperation between the Association of Southeast Asian Nations and the People's Republic of China, Phnom Penh, 4 November 2002. http://www.aseansec.org/13196.htm. Retrieved September 14, 2005.

(3) The Framework Agreement on Comprehensive Economic Co-operation provides for an ASEAN-China Free Trade Area (ACFTA) by the year 2010 only for China and the six wealthier ASEAN countries Brunei Darussalam, Indonesia, Malaysia, the Philippines, Singapore and Thailand. The newer, poorer Member Countries, Cambodia, Laos, Myanmar and Viet Nam have until 2015 to comply.

(4) ASEAN Secretariat (n. d.). ASEAN-China Dialogue Relations. http://www.aseansec.org/5874.htm. Retrieved September 14, 2005.

(5) Grosserman, B., and Fritchi, V. B., Trade pact could trap ASEAN into state of irrelevance. The Japan Times, November 15. 2002.

(6) ASEAN Secretariat (2003). Joint Declaration of the Heads of State/Government of the Association of Southeast Asian Nations and the People's Republic of China on Strategic Partnership for Peace and Prosperity, Bali, 8 October 2003. http://www.aseansec.org/15265.htm. Retrieved September 14, 2005.

(7) White Paper on International trade in 2001 focused on China's economic growth and its impacts on Japan and the East Asia.

(8) The Straits Times, November 7, 2001

(9) MOFA, Japan (2002), Speech by Prime Minister of Japan Junichiro Koizumi, Japan and ASEAN in East Asia: A sincere and Open Partnership, January 14, 2002, Singapore.

(10) Joint Declaration of Leaders of Japan on the Comprehensive Economic Partnership, in Phnom Penh, Cambodia on the 5th November, article 4.

(11) The Japan Times, October 9, 2003

(12) The Asahi Shim bun, November, 2004
(13) Hook, Glenn D. (2000), 'Globalization, East Asian Regionalization, and Japan's Role in Euro-Asian Inter-regionalization', Japan Review, No. 12, pp 5-40.
(14) Yun, C. (2002) "Japan's FTA strategy and the East Asian economic bloc', translated from Sekai 699 (March 2002), http://www.iwanami.co.jp [18 March 2002].
(15) Soesastro, Hadi (2000), "ASEAN 2030: The Long View", in Simon SC Tay et el (eds.), A New ASEAN in a New Millennium (Jakarta: Center for Strategic and International Studies), pp. 187-227.
(16) Far Eastern Economic Review, 'Battered But Still on Top', January 24, 2002, p24.
(17) The Strait Times, 4 November, 2002.
(18) Far Eastern Economic Review "Nothing's Free", 31 October 2002.
(19) The First ASEAN Economic Ministers and the Minister of India Consultation, 15 September 2002, Bandar Seri Begwan, Brunei Darussalam, Paragraph6, 7.
(20) The Japan Times, November 15, 2002.
(21) Keynote Address by Sathirathai, Surakiart (2003), Minister of Foreign Affairs of Thailand, at the Asia Pacific Forum, Berlin, Federal Republic of Germany, 19 September 2003. Also see Framework Agreement for Thai-India FTA, 10 October 2003.
(22) See Polidano, Charles (2000), 'Measuring Public Sector Capacity', World Development 28, no. 5, pp. 805-22.
(23) Luce, Edward and Thornhill, John (2001), 'East Asia Seeks its Own Voice, Financial Times, 14 May 2001, p.20.
(24) Strange, Susan (1998), Mad Money: When Markets Outgrow Government (Ann Arbor: University of Michigan Press), pp23-39.
(25) John Ravenhill (2002), op.cit., Vol 2, pp 175-178.
(26) Richard Stubbs, op. cit. pp 450-454.
(27) Quoted in Castellano (2000), who provides further discussion of the various proposals, 'East Asian monetary union: more than just talk?' Japan Economic Institute Report, no.12, 24 March.
(28) Waltz, Kenneth (1979) Theory of International Politics, New York: Random House. Pp 45-59.
(29) Friedberg, Aaron L. (1993/94) 'Ripe for rivalry: prospects for peace in a multipolar Asia', International Security, 18(3): 5-33.
(30) Keohane, Robert (1984), 'After Hegemony: Cooperation and Discord in the World Political Economy', Princeton: Princeton University Press, Ruggie, John G (ed) (1993) Multilaterism Matters: The Theory and Praxis of an Institutional Form, New York: Columbia University Press.
(31) There are five stages in the economic integration. 1.The tariff and the quantity limit in the region are abolished. "Free Trade Agreements (FTA)" 2.The tariff to the external is unified. "Tariff Union" 3.The factor of production's movement is liberalized. "Common Market" 4.The economic policy is adjusted. "Economic Union" 5.The economic policies are united by setting up a super-state organ. "Complete Economic Union"

These five stages are based on the classification of international economy scholar B. Barassa often quoted. However, this stage theory that he announced in 1962 doesn't necessarily apply to the advanced economic integration.

Chapter 9 Conclusion

In this thesis, firstly I considered the theoretical history of international political economy in order to the theoretical stream toward the current regionalization and globalization. Then I examined the regionalism in East Asia which dose not oppose to globalism and the actor in regionalism is diverse. I also examined the theoretical background of the regionalism in East Asia. These three theoretical back bones are the most important points in order to view the current East Asian regionalism. It was beneficial to compare the regional cooperation with the case of European Union to predict the future of East Asian regional cooperation. Finally, I suggested the appropriate way of East Asian regional cooperation with considering new world system.

As I noted, the Asian economic crisis has spurred the steady deepening of interdependence between East Asian countries and Japan, while Japanese companies in Asia are reshaping their management strategies to meet the challenges of the changing economic circumstances. Where the market has led the way to date in deepening interdependence in Asia, new directions are now beginning to emerge, as seen in research among industrial, academic and government experts on a possible free trade agreement between Japan and Singapore, as well as private-sector studies by research institutes on a Japan-Korea FTA.

In terms of world trends, the number of regional groupings grew in the 1990s, while the shape of integration also developed from trade liberalization through tariff reductions to "deeper integration" reaching as far as the harmonization of domestic systems. Examining the economic significance of regional integration and observing developments in the EU, NAFTA and other regional groupings will be valuable in charting the road ahead for East Asian regional integration.

Regional financial cooperation in East Asia is still in its infancy. Institutions and initiatives are not sufficiently developed for significant regional economic integration.

Nonetheless, some important steps have been taken. The CMI is dealing with the issues of regional liquidity support, and several forums have been created for information sharing, policy dialogue and economic surveillance among the financial authorities. As yet, there have been no visible steps towards exchange rate stabilization or for macroeconomic policy coordination. East Asian countries maintain open regionalism in the global system governed by the WTO, the IMF and the World Bank, while keeping close dialogues with the Americas and the European Union.

Further regional cooperation will require freer movements of goods, services and labor;

convergence of per capita incomes, economic structures and systems, and institutions; and creation of a sound financial system and development of deeper capital markets. A stronger surveillance process is essential not only for better information sharing and policy dialogue, but also for in-depth understanding of the region's economies, more effective policymaking to avoid crises, and better responses to a crisis once it breaks out. The CMI could lead to the creation of a more formal, reserve pooling institution; then minimizing the moral hazard problem would be an important challenge for the region. A framework for exchange rate and monetary policy coordination will have to be developed.

Regional financial cooperation in East Asia is unlikely to be of a North American type, where a US-centered, asymmetric approach has driven regional joint initiatives-mainly in trade and investment liberalization. For East Asia, a European-style, symmetric approach would be more realistic. Japan and China are big powers in Asia, but neither is dominant.

Regional financial cooperation can be beneficial to all economies given the potential for dynamic economic growth and the availability of abundant financial resources. Japan, China and South Korea and ASEAN must work jointly towards further financial cooperation in the region. Strong political will and a vision for regional integration will be required for such endeavors.

But, there are also many problems which should be solved toward the regional cooperation such as a security problem between China and Taiwan and North Korea. Especially, if I limit the problem for regional financial and monetary cooperation, Chinese monetary policy would be one of the most important issues.

Because Chinese exports have such a large imported-input component, the impact of appreciation is likely to be less than in many other countries. To the extent that the argument here is for an exchange rate that is gradually permitted to fluctuate more freely rather than for a substantial step revaluation of the currency, the short-run impact on exports will be smaller still.

There would presumably be a slight decline in the rate of growth concentrated in periods when the Chinese economy threatened to overheat, but this would be a welcome manifestation of heightened stability. There would be some shift from the production of traded to non-traded goods and a somewhat greater tendency for Chinese firms to move toward the production of more skilled-labor intensive, technologically-sophisticated goods, none of which is obviously unwelcome. If the shift to the new exchange rate regime is completed in timely fashion, there is no reason to think that these changes would be overly disruptive.

This in turn suggests that the impact on other Asian countries will not be overwhelming.

But those effects will be diverse: they will be modestly positive for the region's low income economies and modestly negative for its high income countries. Insofar as the competitiveness of the two sets of economies is affected in opposite directions, the pressure on their currencies and the desirable direction of exchange rate adjustment will similarly be different. From this point of view, it makes no sense to attempt to manage Asian exchange rates in the wake of the change in Chinese policy so as to prevent intra-regional fluctuations.

Bibliography (Foreign Books)

Alnert, M	Capilatism versus Capitalism, Whurr (1995)
Annan, Kofi	*Address of Secretary-General Annan to the WorldEconomic Forum in Davos, Switzerland (January 31)'* ,UN Press Release(1999)
Anne O Krueger	Trading Policies and Developing Nations, Brookings, (1995)
Axelrod, R.	The Evolution of Cooperation, Basic Books (1984)
Balassa, B	The theory of Economic Integration, Irwin (1996)
Baldwin, Robert E.	The Political Economy of U.S. Import Policy, Cambridge, MASS (1985)
Baldwin, Robert E.	Trade Policy Issues and Empirical Analysis. University of Chicago press (1988)
Bandow, D.	*Kill the IMF,* Fortune, 25 March: 40 (1998)
Barratt Brown, M.	The Economics of Imperialism, Penguin (1974)
Biersteker, Thomas J	*The Triumph of Neoclassical Economics,* in Rosenau and Czempiel (eds.), pp.102-31(1992)
Bressand, A.	The Euro at the Vanguard of Global Integration, Prométhée (1998)
Brown, C.	International Relations Theory: *New Normative Approaches,* Harvester Wheatsheaf (1992)
Bull, H.	The Anarchical Society: *A Study of Order in World Politics,* Macmillan (1997)
Butterfield, H.	History and Human Relations, Collins (1951)
Buzan, B.	People, States and Fear, Harvester Wheatsheaf (1991)
Cable, V	Globalization and Global Governance, Royal Institute of International Affairs (1999)
Cable, V	The World's New Fissures: *Indentities in Crisis,* Demos (1994)
Carr, E.H.	The Twenty Years Crisis, 1919-1939, London, Macmillan (1981)
Carr, E.H.	The New Society, Macmillan (1951)
Carr, E.H.	What is History, Macmillan (1961)
Casson, M.	Multinationals and World Trade, Allen and Unwin (1986)
Castellano, Marc	*East Asian Monetary Union: More Than Just Talk?,* in: Japan Economic Institute Report, No. 12A (2000)
Chatterjee, P. and Finger, M.	The Earth Brokers, Routledge (1994)
Cohen,B.J.	The Question of Imperialism: *The Political Economy od Dominance and Dependence,* London, Macmillan (1974)
Cooper, R.	The Post Modern State and the World Order, Domos (1996)
Cox, R.W.	*Gramsci, Hegemony and International Relations: An Essay in Methode,* Millennium: Journal of International Studies, vol.12
Cox, R.W.	The New Realism: *Perspectives on Multilateralism and World Order,* Macmillan/ United Nations University Press
Cox, R.W.	Production, Power and World Order, Colunbia U.P. (1987)
Dobson, A.	Green Political Thought, Routledge (1990)

Drucker, P.F.	The New Realities, Mandarin (1990)
Dunning, J.	The Globalisation of Business, Routledge (1993)
Eckersley, R.	Environmentalism and Political Theory, UCL Press (1992)
Eichengreen, B.	The International Monetary System for 21st Century, Brookings Institution (1995)
Eichengreen, B.	Golden Fetters, Oxford U.P. (1992)
Eichengreen, B.	Globalizing Capital, Princeton U.P. (1996)
Eichengreen, B. and Mussa, A.	*Capital Account Liberalization: Theoretical and Proctical Aspects'*, IMF Occasional Paper 172. (1998)
Emmanuel, A.	Unequal Exchange: A study of the Imperialism of Trade, New Left Books (1972)
F Cainrncross	Costing the Earth, Business Books/The economic books, (1991)
Friedman, M.	Essays in Positive Economics, University of Chicafo Press (1953)
Gilbert, E. and Helleiner, E.	Nation-States and Money, Routledge (1999)
Gill, S. and Law, D.	The Global Political Economy, Harvester Wheatsheaf (1988)
Gill, Stephen	American Hegemony and the Trilateral Commission, Cambridge University Press (1990)
Gill, Stephen	Globalisation, Democratisation and Multilateralism, Macmillan/United Nations University Press (1997)
Gill, Stephen	Gramsci, Historcal Materialism and International Relations, Cambridge U.P. (1993)
Gilpin, R	The Plitical Economy of Intewrnational Relations, Princeton U.P. (1987)
Gilpin, R	The political Economy Of International Relations, Princeton U.P.
Goldsmith, J	The Trap, Macmillan (1996)
Gray, J.	Neyond the New Right, Routledge (1993)
Griffiths, M.	Realism, Idealism and International Politics: a Reinterpreation, Routledge (1992)
Grossman, G. and Helpman, E.	Innovation and Growth in the Global Economy, MIT Press (1991)
Guha, R.	The Unquiet Woods, O.U.P.
H Daly, and R Goodland	*An Ecological-Economic Assessment of Deregulation of international Commerce under GATT*, World Bank, Sept (1992)
Hardin, G	*The tragedy of the commons*, Science 162: 1243-8 (1968)
Harry G Jonson	Economic Policies toward Less Developed Countries, Brookings, (1967)
Helleiner, E.	The Making of National Money, Cornell U.P. (2003)
Henderson, D.	The MAI Affair: A story and its Lessons, RIIA (1999)
Hughes, Christopher R.	*Nationalism and multilateralism in Chinese Foreign policy: implications for Southeast Asia*, The Pocific Review, 18:1 (March 2005): 119-135
ILO	Multinational Enterprises and Employment, ILO,(1988)
James, H.	International Monetary Cooperation since Bretton Woods, Oxford University Press (1996)
James, W.	A Pluralistic Universe, Harvard U.P. (1977)

Jervis, R.	Perception and Misperceotion in International Politics, Princeton U.P. (1976)
JK Galbraith	The Culture of Contentment, Sinclaire Stevenson, (1992)
Johnson, H.	The New Mercantilism: Some Problems in International Trade, Money and Investment, Blackwell (1974)
Jones, B.	*Globalization versus Community,* New Political Economy, Vol.2, No.1. (1997)
Keohane, Robert	After Hegemony, Princeton U.P. (1984)
Keohane, Robert and Joseph Nye	Transnational Relations and World Politics, Harvard University Press (1972)
Kindleberger, C.	Power and Money, Macmillan (1973)
Kindleberger, C.	*International Public Goods without International Government,* American Economic Review (1986)
Krugman, P.	Strategic Trade Policy in New International Economics, MIT Press (1986)
Krugman, P.	*Regionalism versus Multilateralism,* in J. De Melo and A. Panagariya, *New Dimensions in Regional Integration,* CEPR (1993)
Krugman, P.	*Does Third World Growth Hurt First World Prosperity?,* Harvard Business Review, July/August, pp.113-21 (1994)
Krugman, P.	*Growing World Trade: Causes and Consequences.,* Brooking Papers on Economic Activity, No.1. (1995)
Krugman, P. and Lawrence, R.	*Trade, Jobs and Wages.,* NBER Working Paper 4478, (1993)
Lang, T. and Hines, C.	The New Protectionism, Earthscan Publications (1993)
Lardy, N.	Foreign Trade and Reform in China 1978-9, Cambridge University Press (1992)
Lardy, N.	China and the World Economy, Institute for International Economics (1994)
Lukes, S.	Power: a Radical View, Macmillan (1974)
Luttwak, E.	*Where Are the Great Powers?,* Foreign Affairs, July/August (1994)
Marx, K.	A Contribution to the Critique of Political Economy, Lawrence & Wishart (1970)
Merchant, C.	Radical Ecology, Routledge (1992)
Mundell, R.	*The Theory of Optimum Currency Areas,* American Economic Review (1961)
Murphy, C.	International Organization and Industrial Change, Polity Press (1994)
Nicolaides, P.	*Competition Amoung Rules,* World Competition: Law and Economics Review (1992)
O'Brien, R.	Global Financial Interpretation: The End of Geography, RIIA/Pinter (1992)
Paul, L.	Who Elected the Bankers?, Cornell U.P. (1997)
Polanyi, Karl	The Great Transformation, Beacon Press (1957)
Redclift, M.	Sustainable Development, Routledge (1987)
Reich, R.	The Work of Nations, Vintage (1992)
Robertson Roland	Globalization Social Theory and Global Culture, SAGE Publications (1992)
Strange, Susan	Protectionism and World Politics, International Organization (1985),
Strange, Susan	The Retreat of the State: The Diffusion of Power in the World Economy, Cambridge University Press (1996)

Strange, Susan	States and Markets, Pinter. (1988)
Taylor, M.	Anarchy and Cooperation, Wiley (1976)
Tobin, J.	Speculator's Tax, New Economy (1994)
Tumer, P.	*Capital Flows in the 1980s,* BIS Economic Papers No.3 (1991)
Underhill, G.	New World Order in International Finance, Macmillan (1996)
Wallerstein, I	Unthinking Social Science, Polity. (1991)
Walter, A.	World Money/World Power, Harvester Wheatsheaf (1993)
Waltz, K.N.	Theory os International Politics, Reading, MA & London, Addison-Wesley (1979)
Waters, M.	Globalization, Routledge (1995)
Williamson, J.	The Exchange Rate System, Institute for International Economics (1995)
Zheng, Joan	*China: Domestic Reverberations of the Renminbi Peg,* J. P. Morgan Global Data Watch, 19 September pp.11-13. (2003a)
Zheng, Joan	*China's Export Surge Reflects Structural Trends,* J.P. Morgan Global Data Watch, 13 June, pp.19-20. (2003b)

Bibliography (Japanese Books)

青木 健	『AFTA(ASEAN自由貿易地域)―ASEAN経済統合の実状と展望』日本貿易振興会、2001年。
秋山憲治	『アメリカ通商政策と貿易摩擦』同文舘出版、1990年。
秋山憲治	『貿易政策と国際通商関係』同文舘出版、1998年。
天野明弘	『貿易論』筑摩書房、1986年。
石見 徹	『開発と環境の政治経済学』東京大学出版会、2004年。
石山嘉英	『通貨金融危機と国際マクロ経済学』日本評論社、2004年。
伊藤元重/著 大山道広/著	『国際貿易』岩波書店、1985年。
伊藤元重/編 奥野正寛/編	『通商問題の政治経済学』日本経済新聞社、1991年。
今井譲	『マネタリズムの政策と理論』東洋経済新報社、1984年。
イマニュエル・ウォーラーステイン/山田鋭夫他訳	『世界システムの方法』藤原書店、2002年。
岩井克人	『貨幣論』筑摩書房、1993年。
内田和男	『経済不均衡と貨幣』勁草書房、1988年。
円居総一	「情報化と企業・産業組織の構造変化―グローバルスタンダードの本質と政策的課題―」国際関係研究所『国際関係研究』日本大学国際関係学部、2002年第22巻第4号。
円居総一	『国際収支の経済学』有斐閣、1994年。
遠藤 正寛	『地域貿易協定の経済分析』東京大学出版会、2005年。
大久保隆	『マネーサプライと金融政策 理論と実証』東洋経済新報社、1983年。
大矢根聡	「東アジアFTA：日本の政策転換と地域構想」『国際問題』2004年3月号 No. 528
岡本磐男	『管理通貨制とインフレ機構』有斐閣、1983年。

奥田宏司	『ドル体制とユーロ、円』日本経済評論社、2002年。
小野朝男	『金・外国為替・国際金融』ダイヤモンド社、1986年。
小野善康	『貨幣経済の動学理論 ケインズの復権』東京大学出版会、1992年。
尾上修悟	『国際金融論 グローバル金融危機の構造』ミネルヴァ書房、2003年。
嘉治佐保子	『国際通貨体制の経済学―ユーロ・アジア・日本―』日本経済新聞社、2004年。
片岡尹	『ドル本位制の通貨危機 国際資金ポンプとしての米国』勁草書房、2001年。
加藤隆俊	『円・ドル・元 為替を動かすのは誰か』東洋経済新報社、2002年。
金谷貞男	『貨幣経済学』新世社、1992年。
ガレット・ハーディン/竹内靖雄訳	『サバイバル・ストラテジー』思索社、1983年。
菊地悠二	『人民元は世界の脅威か 円・ドル・元の競争と戦略』時事通信出版局、2005年。
国宗浩三	『アジア諸国金融改革の論点 「強固な」金融システムを目指して』日本貿易振興会アジア経済研究所、2001年。
公文俊平	『情報化社会序説－ラストモダンの時代を生きる』NTT出版、2004年。
公文俊平	『社会システム論』日本経済新聞社、1978年。
公文俊平	『文明の進化と情報化』NTT出版、2001年。
黒田東彦	『通貨外交 財務官の1300日』東洋経済新報社、2003年。
黒田東彦	『通貨の興亡―円、ドル、ユーロ、人民元の行方』中央公論新社、2005年。
黒田東彦	『元切り上げ』日経BP社、2004年。
後藤健二	『欧州通貨統合は何を克服したのか ドイツから見た1995年～1999年』大蔵財務協会、2001年。
小林通	『現代国際経済システムの原点と構図』時潮社、2001年。
小林通	『東アジア経済圏構想と国際分業』高文堂出版社、2006年。
佐伯啓思	『アダムスミスの誤算 幻想のグローバル資本主義（上）』PHP新書、1999年。
佐伯啓思	『ケインズの予言 幻想のグローバル資本主義（下）』PHP新書、1999年。
坂田幹男	『北東アジア経済論 経済交流圏の全体像』ミネルヴァ書房、2001年。
志水誠	『マコトアプローチ 円高が進行しない本当の理由とアジア通貨の比較分析』文芸社、2002年。
白井早由里	『人民元と中国経済』日本経済新聞社、2004年。
白井早由里	『カレンシーボードの経済学』日本評論社、2000年。
宿輪 純一	『アジア金融システムの経済学』日本経済新聞社、2006年。
進藤 榮一	『東アジア共同体を設計する』日本経済評論社、2006年。
添谷 芳秀	『日本の東アジア構想』慶應義塾大学出版会、2004年。
田中明彦	『新しい中世 相互依存深まる世界システム』日経ビジネス人文庫、2003年。
田中明彦	『新しい「中世」21世紀の世界システム』日本経済新聞社、1996年。
田中明彦	『世界システム』東京大学出版会、1989年。
田中五郎	『国際通貨制度の改革』日本評論社、2002年。
田中素香/藤田誠一編著	『ユーロと国際通貨システム』蒼天社出版、2003年。
田中素香	『EMS・欧州通貨制度―欧州通貨統合の焦点』有斐閣、1996年。
谷口 誠	『東アジア共同体―経済統合のゆくえと日本』岩波書店、2004年。
唐成	『中国の貯蓄と金融 家計・企業・政府の実証分析』慶応義塾大学出版会、2005年。

西口 清勝編著	『東アジア共同体の構築』ミネルヴァ書房、2006年。
根本忠宣	『基軸通貨の政治経済学』学文社、2003年。
福田 慎一 編, 小川 英治 編	『国際金融システムの制度設計 通貨危機後の東アジアへの教訓』東京大学出版会、2006年。
本多健吉	『世界経済システムと南北関係』新評論、2001年。
松井 均	『銀行原理と国際通貨システム』勁草書房、2002年。
松浦一悦	『EU通貨統合の新展開』ミネルヴァ書房、2005年。
森嶋通夫	『日本にできることは何か 東アジア共同体を提案する』岩波書店、2001年。
山下英次	『ヨーロッパ通貨統合 その成り立ちとアジアへのレッスン』勁草書房、2002年。
山本栄治/著 西村閑也/編集	『国際通貨と国際資金循環』日本経済評論社、2002年。

川戸　秀昭　Hideaki Kawato

略　歴　1974年千葉生まれ。日本大学国際関係学部卒業、日本大学大学院国際関係研究科修了、英国 Warwick 大学大学院国際政治経済学科修了、日仏共同博士課程派遣留学（パリ第一大学大学院経済学部）、日本大学大学院国際関係研究科博士後期課程修了。博士（国際関係）
現在、日本大学短期大学部商経学科助教。

Theoretical Background of Asian Regionalizationand
the Changing of the World System

HIDEAKI KAWATO

Professor, and Dr. of Eng., College of International Relations, Nihon Junior College

Copyright © 2007 by Jichosha Inc. Tokyo, JAPAN

First edition : July 2007

ISBN-978-4-7888-0620-7